★ American G

Character Encyclopedia

Written by Carrie Anton
and Erin Falligant

★ American Girl
Character
Encyclopedia

Contents

Chapter 1
American Girl® characters

Whether starring in stories from the past
or from today, these characters inspire
girls to dream big and make a difference.

KAYA™

Round hair ties

An adventurous girl, Kaya is a friend to the earth and animals. She dreams of becoming a courageous leader of her tribe, the Nez Perce. Kaya draws strength from her family, who help her prepare for whatever the future brings.

ALL ABOUT ME

★ Full name: **Kaya'aton'my'**

★ Name meaning: **She Who Arranges Rocks** (in Nez Perce)

★ Favorite activities: **Riding her horse, caring for animals, and swimming**

★ Favorite stories: **Grandmother's**

Furry friend

Kaya's dog, Tatlo, sticks by her side when she gathers food. Kaya places what she finds into a woven basket.

Moccasin booties

In This Year...

European settlers have not yet traveled as far as the Pacific Northwest, where the Nez Perce live.

Kaya's world

In the summer, Kaya and the Nez Perce people travel to find food, sleeping in tepees. In the winter, they live in permanent shelters called longhouses. The tribe celebrates its culture with singing, dancing, and feasts.

Tepee shelter

Embroidered belt

Moveable shelter
Kaya's tepee is a cozy place to sleep. It is easy to pack up and carry when traveling with her tribe.

Winter wear
In the cold winter months, Kaya bundles up in layers of clothing, long mittens, and a furry hood.

Fringed dress

FELICITY MERRIMAN™

Wide-brimmed straw hat

Floral embroidered gown

Felicity is growing up in colonial Williamsburg, Virginia, just before the start of the American Revolution, a war that sees America break away from British rule. Adventurous Felicity is never afraid to stand up for what she believes in.

Gala gown

Even though she doesn't always enjoy dressing in ladylike clothes, Felicity is excited to go to the holiday ball. She wears a festive dress for the occasion.

ALL ABOUT ME

★ Nickname: **Lissie**

★ Favorite animal: **Horse**

★ Likes: **Horseback riding and playing with best friend Elizabeth**

★ Dislikes: **Embroidery, cooking, and dancing**

DID YOU KNOW?
Felicity's grandfather owned many horses, and he taught Felicity how to ride.

Felicity's world

For girls Felicity's age, "proper" pastimes include cooking, sewing, and dancing. But Felicity has an adventurous spirit and prefers exploring the outdoors while riding her horse, Penny.

Pattens

Fingerless mitts

Warm winter cloak

Lacy pinner cap

Winter warmers

In winter, Felicity keeps warm by putting on her mitts and slipping her hands inside an embroidered muff. She ties pattens to her shoes to keep her feet out of mud and puddles.

In This Year...

Many colonists, known as Patriots, want to break away from British rule. They begin planning how to gain independence.

In the stables

Felicity loves taking care of Penny's foal, Patriot. At night, she covers him with a cozy blanket to keep him warm.

ELIZABETH COLE™

Pierced ears

Coral pink taffeta gown

Born in England, Elizabeth is now growing up in Virginia. Her family are Loyalists, meaning that they want America to remain under British rule. Her best friend Felicity's family are Patriots who want America to become independent. Politics may divide Elizabeth and Felicity's families, but Elizabeth remains loyal to her good friend.

ALL ABOUT ME

★ Family nickname: **Bitsy**

★ Favorite lesson: **Sewing**

★ Secret wish: **To be as brave as Felicity**

★ Favorite pastime: **Poking fun at older sister Annabelle**

A proper young lady

Elizabeth and Felicity take classes to learn to dance, serve tea, and do fancy stitching and handwriting. They also learn how to curtsy to show respect when they meet someone important.

In This Year...

War is brewing. Patriots, unlike Loyalists, don't want to pay taxes to the king of England for things such as tea.

Elizabeth's world

For Elizabeth, life in Virginia feels very different from her old life in England. Teatime, however, feels the same, and with Felicity by her side, Elizabeth begins to feel at home.

Wooden tea caddy

Sugar bowl

Teatime gown

Time for tea
Elizabeth learns how to carefully measure the tea into the teapot. She then fills the teacups without spilling a drop!

DID YOU KNOW?
Elizabeth loves dancing! She dreams of attending a dance at the royal Governor's Palace.

Sleep tight
Elizabeth's home is large and elegant, but it can get chilly! She wears slippers to keep her toes toasty, and her four-poster bed has curtains to keep in warmth.

CAROLINE ABBOTT™

Bonnet

Brave Caroline dreams of being the captain of her own ship, like her father. Her spirit is tested when war comes to her hometown and she has to help rescue her father from the British enemy.

Sailing

Caroline's papa repairs a small sailboat that has been damaged in the war. He names the two-seater boat "Miss Caroline" and paints the name on the side.

In This Year...

The War of 1812 between the U.S. and Great Britain begins. The war lasts for three years, when both sides agree to make peace.

Hem trimmed with tucks

ALL ABOUT ME

★ Hometown: **Sackets Harbor, New York**

★ Favorite activities: **Sailing, fishing, and sewing**

★ Least favorite chore: **Baking**

★ Pet: **A black cat named Inkpot**

Caroline's world

Caroline's family runs a shipyard near Lake Ontario. Caroline loves being out on the water—whether it's sailing in the summer or ice-skating in the winter.

Braided hairpiece

On the lake
Caroline loves to glide along the frozen lake on her ice skates. Her blue coat with fur trim keeps her warm.

Brocade chair seats

Floral-detailed stripes

Happy birthday!
It's hard to get supplies during the war. For her birthday, Caroline is given a special treat of applesauce cake to enjoy around the table with her family.

DID YOU KNOW?
Caroline is an only child. She has no brothers or sisters.

JOSEFINA MONTOYA™

My year is **1824**

Josefina lives on a New Mexican farm called a rancho. Ever since Mamá died, Josefina has tried to preserve her mother's traditions. But so much is changing! American traders arrive in New Mexico with new ideas. Josefina bravely faces these changes with hope.

Golden hoop earrings

Feast day

Instead of a birthday, Josefina celebrates the feast day of San José, the saint she was named after. She wears her mother's shawl and carries her lace fan.

ALL ABOUT ME

★ Favorite flower: **Primrose**

★ Pet: **A baby goat named Sombrita**

★ Best friend: **Mariana**

★ Activities: **Sewing, playing piano, and picking herbs and flowers**

Rebozo, or shawl

DID YOU KNOW?
Josefina wants to be a healer. She makes a paste from a special plant to treat her friend's rattlesnake bite.

Soft moccasins with laces

Josefina's world

Josefina spends most of her time at home on the rancho, helping to weave, garden, bake, and care for the animals. She also enjoys visiting the busy markets in Santa Fe.

Straw hat with braided trim

Weaving

Josefina weaves on a Navajo Indian loom. She makes blankets and shawls for her family.

Strap tightens under chin!

Ruffled calico riding dress

In This Year...

New Mexico is still part of Mexico, not the United States. But Americans visit Santa Fe to trade goods for the first time.

Fiesta!

Parties call for fancy clothing and delicious food. Josefina helps her family bake outdoors in an *horno*, or clay oven.

CÉCILE REY

Velvet-trimmed hat with rosette

My year is 1853

Cécile comes from a well-to-do family in New Orleans. She loves parties, but she makes time for helping others, too. Cécile enjoys volunteering at an orphanage, visiting the elderly, and teaching her friend Marie-Grace to speak French.

ALL ABOUT ME

★ Best friend: **Marie-Grace**

★ Favorite snack: **Pralines (sweet treats made with pecan nuts, cream, and sugar)**

★ Favorite hobbies: **Charades, reciting poems, and acting out plays**

★ Dreams for the future: **To be a stage actress and to travel the world**

In the parlor

Cécile sits at her desk to write letters to her older brother, Armand. He's been studying in Paris, France, for two years. She misses him very much.

In This Year...

There are many free people of color in New Orleans in 1853. They have more education and opportunities than black people anywhere else in the United States.

Cécile's world

Confident Cécile loves being in the spotlight. Whether it's putting on a pretend performance or dancing at a party, Cécile always shines.

Velvet hair ribbons

Clever pet

Cécile finds that her parrot, Cochon, has a gift for speaking! He mimics her words, especially if she rewards him with pecan nuts.

Desk with hidden seat

DID YOU KNOW?
Cécile sings off-key! She'd much rather act out plays or recite poetry than sing a song in front of an audience.

Posy print dress

Costume ball

In Cécile's time, balls for white people and black people are separated. She and Marie-Grace decide to wear the same masked costume so they can switch places and attend both balls.

MARIE-GRACE GARDNER

Shy Marie-Grace returns to New Orleans after four years away—but so much has changed! She worries that she will never make new friends and feel at home again.

DID YOU KNOW?
Marie-Grace has two nicknames. Her mother called her "Ti-Marie," and the children she visits at the orphanage call her "Marie-the-Great."

Golden heart-shaped locket

Fan for hot days

Summer nights
Hot New Orleans summers bring swarms of mosquitoes. At night, Marie-Grace sleeps beneath a mosquito net to protect herself from bug bites.

ALL ABOUT ME

★ Best friend: **Cécile Rey**

★ Best furry friend: **Argos, her shaggy dog**

★ Favorite activities: **Helping Papa at his doctor's office and exploring the open-air market**

★ Special talents: **Singing, arithmetic, and entertaining children**

Marie-Grace's world

Adjustable mirror

Marie-Grace's worries about fitting in are over when she meets Cécile. Her outgoing new friend helps Marie-Grace feel confident and inspires her to help others by volunteering at an orphanage.

Fashionable ringlets

Getting ready

Marie-Grace washes up at her vanity stand and adds a splash of perfume—either lavender or rosewater. She's ready to volunteer at the orphanage.

Sateen jacket with ribbons

In This Year...

A yellow fever outbreak leads to many deaths in New Orleans and other parts of Louisiana. Yellow fever is carried by mosquitoes.

Striped skirt over pantalettes

Under the sun

Marie-Grace and Cécile have lots of fun together in the vibrant city of New Orleans. They use parasols to protect themselves from the bright sun.

KIRSTEN LARSON™

Gingham-check sun bonnet

When Kirsten moves to America from Sweden with her family, she feels like she will never belong in her new home. But Kirsten wants to be brave like her mother and she tries her hardest to make the best of her new life.

Home sweet home

Kirsten wears an embroidered apron from Sweden to bake Swedish treats. Celebrating her traditions makes her feel less homesick.

DID YOU KNOW?

Kirsten had a hard time fitting in at school at first, but she soon made friends.

Blue calico dress

ALL ABOUT ME

★ Born in: **Ryd, Sweden**

★ Lives in: **Minnesota Territory**

★ Favorite toy: **Sari, her rag doll**

★ Hobbies: **Exploring the outdoors, sewing, and baking**

Kirsten's world

In Minnesota, Kirsten and her family mix old traditions with new ones. One of Kirsten's favorite Swedish holiday traditions is Saint Lucia Day, celebrated on the darkest day of the year.

Floral-painted details

Saint Lucia wreath

Mix it up

Swedish and American treats combine to make an extra-special Christmas feast in Kirsten's new home of Minnesota.

Woven table runner

In This Year...

Just like Kirsten and her family, many people move from Europe and the East Coast of America to settle on the frontier.

Lace-trimmed Saint Lucia gown

Old and new

In her brand-new bed, Kirsten cuddles her old rag doll that she brought with her from Sweden. Her new school friends made this colorful quilt just for Kirsten.

ADDY WALKER™

Addy is a courageous girl growing up during the Civil War. After she and her mother escape from slavery in the South to start a new life in Philadelphia, she dreams of reuniting with her father, brother, and baby sister. Addy always holds onto her hope for better days ahead.

Golden hoop earrings

ALL ABOUT ME

★ Favorite school subject: **Spelling**

★ Favorite family recipe: **Momma's sweet potato pudding**

★ Ambition: **To become a teacher**

★ Hobbies: **Jumping rope, gardening, making puppets, and putting on puppet shows**

Lace pantalettes

In This Year...

The Civil War has been going on for three years. The North and the South are divided on whether slavery should be legal.

Bedtime

Winter is chilly in the tiny attic where Addy and Momma live in Philadelphia. Addy is thankful for her flannel nightgown and cozy quilt.

Addy's world

Even in hard times, Addy's family makes time for fun, such as going to the church's summer fair and celebrating birthdays and holidays together.

A special day

Addy doesn't know her actual birthday, so she chooses one. She picks April 9, the day the war ends. This way, the whole country celebrates with her!

Tiny berry brooch

Table set for birthday celebration

Holiday gifts

Addy works at Mrs. Ford's dress shop to earn money for a gift for Momma. She receives a gift, too: a plaid dress to wear on Christmas Day.

SAMANTHA PARKINGTON™

My year is 1904

Samantha is growing up under the care of her wealthy grandmother. They live in a time of great change, with new ideas and inventions altering the way people live. Still, Samantha can see that times aren't good for everyone. She tries to help others less fortunate.

Private lessons

Samantha's friend Nellie O'Malley is working as a servant next door and can't go to school. Samantha teaches Nellie to read and write.

ALL ABOUT ME

★ Best friend: **Nellie O'Malley**

★ Favorite ice cream flavor: **Peppermint**

★ Likes: **Painting, paper dolls, ice-skating, and helping others**

★ Dislikes: **Practicing piano and embroidery**

Velvety burgundy purse

Black Mary Jane shoes

In This Year...

Only men are allowed to vote. Brave women called suffragists fight hard to change that law.

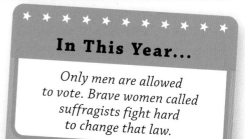

Samantha's world

Samantha likes to paint, just as her mother did. Summer trips to Piney Point, Grandmary's summer home in the mountains, give Samantha plenty of inspiration.

Straw hat with ribbon

Pretty picture

On sunny days, Samantha catches butterflies with a net. When it rains, she "captures" them by painting pictures on Grandmary's covered porch.

Palette and paintbrush

Bike and bloomers

As a "proper young lady," Samantha has to wear dresses every day—except when she rides a bicycle! She loves the freedom of riding in her bloomers.

DID YOU KNOW?
Cars were brand new inventions in 1904. Only wealthy families had one.

Checked bloomers

NELLIE O'MALLEY™

Nellie is working as a servant when she meets Samantha Parkington, who lives next door. When Nellie becomes an orphan, Samantha helps Nellie stay strong as she strives to take care of her younger sisters.

White sunhat with blue ribbon

Bedtime

Nellie loves going to her friend Samantha's house for a sleepover. The girls share stories and secrets late into the night.

★ ALL ABOUT ME ★

- ★ Best friend: **Samantha Parkington**
- ★ Siblings: **Two little sisters, Bridget and Jenny**
- ★ Dream for the future: **To be a teacher**
- ★ Skills: **Sewing, singing, and arithmetic**

Purse holds hankie and Irish penny

DID YOU KNOW?

Nellie's nickname is "Miss Nellie O'Malley-All-Mended," because her father taught her how to repair things—even cars!

Nellie's world

Nellie moves in with Samantha when Samantha's aunt and uncle adopt Samantha, Nellie, and her two sisters. Nellie loves her new life but holds onto treasures from her past.

Hair bow with rhinestones

Finer things

Nellie gets a new wardrobe and fancy accessories when she is adopted. But her prized possession is the cross necklace that belonged to her mother.

Celtic cross necklace

In This Year...

In large cities like New York City, illnesses and factory accidents are common, leaving many children orphaned.

Dolled up

Nellie treasures her porcelain doll Lydia—her first doll ever! Samantha gives Nellie the doll to comfort her during hard times.

Shoes with pink ribbon rosettes

REBECCA RUBIN™

My year is 1914

Rebecca will take on any role that brightens people's lives—from helping a friend to gathering around the Sabbath table with her family. She honors her family's Jewish traditions, and she also loves the latest things, like silent movies!

Shining bright

Hanukkah is Rebecca's favorite time of year! She longs for the day when she can light the candles on her family's treasured menorah, like her older sisters do.

Purse with wrist strap

In This Year...

World War I breaks out in Europe. After that, it is very hard for Jewish families to leave and come to America.

ALL ABOUT ME

★ Family nickname: **Beckie**
★ Favorite book: ***Rebecca of Sunnybrook Farm*** by Kate Douglas Wiggin
★ Favorite subject: **Arithmetic**
★ Hobbies: **Telling jokes, crocheting, singing, and acting**

Rebecca's world

Rebecca wants to be an actress, but her parents want her to do something more traditional, such as teaching. But Rebecca never gives up on her dream.

Director's chair

Taffeta hairbow

Action!
Rebecca is thrilled to visit a movie studio with her cousin Max, where she gets to see a real director's chair, megaphone, and props.

Title cards

Velvet overlay

Through the snow
Winter in New York is pretty—but chilly! When Rebecca walks to her father's shoe store, she stays warm in her velveteen swing coat and matching hat.

DID YOU KNOW?
Rebecca doesn't go to a movie, or "motion picture show," until she's 10.

KIT KITTREDGE™

My year is 1934

When Kit's dad loses his business and her family faces hard times during the Great Depression, Kit puts her creativity to work to make things better. She reaches out to help others and discovers that, even in hard times, hope is always worth holding onto.

Cloche hat with ribbon

A nose for news

Kit is tired of hearing about bad news. So she writes her own newspaper at her attic desk, reporting happier news from around her neighborhood.

In This Year...

America is deep in a financial crisis. Many Americans are without jobs, money, and homes.

Cuff bracelet

ALL ABOUT ME

★ Best friend: **Ruthie Smithens**

★ Dream for the future: **To be a newspaper reporter**

★ Favorite baseball player: **Ernie Lombardi of the Cincinnati Reds**

★ Pet: **A Basset Hound named Grace**

Kit's world

Through challenges and adventures, Kit learns there is more to life than wealth. Even though her family doesn't have much money, Kit knows she has a lot to be grateful for.

Blue cap is a gift from her friend Will

Going to press

Kit types up her news stories on a typewriter. Her news brings a smile to the faces of her readers— her family and their boarders.

Kit's typewriter

Special delivery!

Kit delivers eggs on her scooter to earn extra money. Made from an orange crate and roller skates, the scooter even has room for Kit's dog, Grace.

Kit's brother's old overalls

33

RUTHIE SMITHENS™

Ruthie may be growing up during the Great Depression, but she loves fairy tales and happy endings. She loves her best friend, Kit Kittredge, too. So when she learns that Kit's family is having trouble paying the mortgage on their house, Ruthie searches for ways to make a real-life happy ending come true.

Pitching in

Ruthie ties on an apron and joins Kit on washday. If one girl does the wash while the other irons, chores will be done in half the time!

Watch from her father

In This Year...

President Roosevelt's New Deal is in its second year. This government program was designed to pull America out of the Depression.

Purse and pretty hankie

ALL ABOUT ME

★ Nickname: **Goofy Ruthie**
★ Dream job: **Princess or movie star**
★ Favorite book: *Grimm's Fairy Tales*
★ Favorite place: **Kit's house, because it's full of interesting boarders!**

Ruthie's world

Velvety ribbon headband

Ruthie and Kit find ways to celebrate the good times without spending money. They enjoy holiday baking and throw a "penny-pincher birthday party."

Pink glass pitcher and glasses

Metal table and chairs

Home-grown party

Ruthie loves Kit's penny-pincher party! They decorate the table with fresh flowers from the garden. Kit's Aunt Millie gives the girls lessons in planting seeds, too.

Smocked drop-waist dress

From the heart

Homemade gifts and treats are the perfect way for Ruthie to celebrate the holidays with Kit. They can bake for their families—and for other families in need.

NANEA MITCHELL™

Nanea is a cheerful girl growing up in sunny Hawaii. She loves that the islands are home to people of all kinds. Nanea's Mom is Hawaiian and her Dad moved to Hawaii from Oregon. He works hard as a welder at Pearl Harbor shipyard.

Red hibiscus flower

Cool, sleeveless blouse

ALL ABOUT ME

★ Nickname: **Monkey**

★ Favorite animal: **Her dog, Mele**

★ Likes: **Hula classes and her Mom's guava bread**

★ Dislikes: **Being called "the baby of the family."**

Beach picnic

On Nanea's birthday, her family arranges a picnic on Waikiki Beach. Nanea wears a new skirt in a pineapple print fabric, lovingly sewn by her grandmother.

In This Year...

An attack by Japan on the US naval base at Pearl Harbor, Honolulu, draws the United States into World War II.

Flat sandals

36

Nanea's world

Hawaiian traditions are important to Nanea. She takes hula classes with her Tutu—her grandmother—every Saturday. They always greet each other in the traditional way, by pressing their noses together.

Lei of yellow flowers

Flower garland

Tiny colored lamps

A special feast

On special occasions, Nanea's family celebrates with a feast called a luau. The tasty selection of cooked foods, fresh fruit, and coconut drinks is served on a low wooden table.

DID YOU KNOW?
Nanea's first name is Alice, but her family and friends always call her by her Hawaiian middle name.

Feathered `uli`uli rattle

USO dance

Nanea is practicing a dance for the United Service Organization. She feels very grown up in her holoku dress, with its long train.

MOLLY McINTIRE™

Navy blue beret

A lively, lovable girl, Molly is growing up during World War II. She misses her father, a doctor who is caring for wounded soldiers overseas. She also struggles with the many changes that the war has brought to America. But through her spirit and resourcefulness, Molly is able to find fun in life on the home front.

School days

Molly's teacher, Miss Campbell, says that going to school is Molly's war duty—that being a good student is as important as being a good soldier. Molly tries her best to pay attention and work hard.

Flared skirt

DID YOU KNOW?

Molly dreads multiplication tests. She gets so nervous, she forgets everything she has learned!

★ ALL ABOUT ME ★

- ★ Family nickname: **Olly Molly**
- ★ Best friends: **Linda, Susan, and Emily**
- ★ Best furry friend: **Bennett, a Jack Russell Terrier puppy**
- ★ Lives in: **Jefferson, Illinois**

Molly's world

Celebrating happy occasions, like birthdays, helps Molly take her mind off the war. Molly also loves activities such as school recitals, tap dance classes, and enjoying the great outdoors at summer camp.

Curvy chrome chairs

Birthday tea party

Molly wants an English tea party for her tenth birthday, which she celebrates with her new English friend, Emily. They serve their chocolate cake on elegant china plates.

In This Year...

Some foods, like butter and cocoa, are hard to get during the war. A chocolate birthday cake is a real treat!

Satin school recital outfit

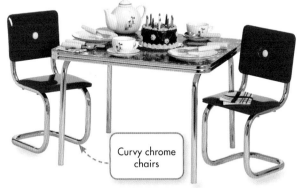

Making camp

At Camp Gowonagain, Molly and her friends sleep in a canvas tent. Molly borrows her dad's flannel sleeping bag to keep her cozy on cool summer nights.

TENT NO. 6

Shiny shoes with bows

EMILY BENNETT™

Cherry-blossom headband

When her home in London, England, is bombed during World War II, Emily's parents send her to America for safety. She stays with Molly McIntire's family. The girls are from different countries, but they have a lot in common. They both love dogs, and they both worry about loved ones during the war.

ALL ABOUT ME

★ Secret wish: **To have curly hair like an English princess**

★ Secret skill: **Identifying fighter planes**

★ Likes: **Helping Molly with math and Mrs. Gilford in the garden**

Pair of pups

Emily and Molly like pretending they're taking their imaginary dogs for walks outside. On Molly's birthday, each girl gets a real terrier puppy.

T-strap shoes

In This Year...

Thousands of British children are evacuated from London during World War II. Many feel homesick during their time away.

Emily's world

Emily tries not to feel homesick, but sometimes it's hard. Her treasures from home comfort her. And Molly cheers her up by teaching her American pastimes, like tap dancing.

World War I identity tags

Home treasures

What reminds Emily of home? The cardigan sweater from Aunt Primrose, a scrapbook of photos, and her grandfather's identity tags from when he was a soldier in World War I.

Snow day

Emily is surprised by how much snow falls in Illinois. She wears a cozy snowsuit to keep warm. Though metal and wood are scarce during the war, she gets to try Molly's old wooden sled.

Tap dance shoes

41

MARYELLEN LARKIN™

Maryellen is always dreaming up big ideas, even though they sometimes get her into trouble. Her wild imagination helps her stand out from the crowd—and from her five brothers and sisters.

Lacy-knit shrug

ALL ABOUT ME

★ Nickname: **Ellie**

★ Siblings: **Joan, Carolyn, Beverly, Tom, and Mikey**

★ Favorite TV shows: **Davy Crockett and The Lone Ranger**

★ Likes: **Drawing, science experiments, and pretending to be a TV heroine**

Winter fun

When she was seven, Maryellen caught polio. The disease made one of her legs weak, but that doesn't stop her from sledding and ice-skating when she visits her grandparents.

Striped dress with full skirt

In This Year...

A new vaccine for polio is invented. Before this, the disease affected millions of people.

Maryellen's world

DID YOU KNOW?
Maryellen's two best friends at school are *both* named Karen.

At school, Maryellen is excited to join the Science Club. She can't wait to build flying machines! Maryellen has an idea for a rocket that's as one-of-a-kind as she is!

Air pump

Model rocket kit

Blast off!
With a kit like this, Maryellen has everything she needs to launch a rocket. But she learns to rely on her teammates, the Loony Balloonies, too.

Bow-print dress

At the diner
The Seaside Diner is Maryellen's favorite place to meet her friends. After school, they talk about TV shows they've watched, dance to popular songs on the jukebox, and enjoy tasty burgers and milkshakes.

MELODY ELLISON™

Melody is chosen to sing a solo at her church in Detroit, but she is nervous. When she hears Dr. Martin Luther King, Jr. speak at a march for freedom, his words inspire her to lift her own voice in support of equality for all people. It takes courage, but she learns each individual voice really can make a difference.

Cowl collar

ALL ABOUT ME

★ Nickname: **Dee-Dee**

★ Best friend: **Her cousin Val**

★ Favorite dessert: **Mommy's triple-chocolate cake**

★ Hobbies: **Singing and gardening**

Bows on side pleats

DID YOU KNOW?
Melody pretends she's a star, singing into her hairbrush like a microphone. But she's actually scared to sing alone in front of a crowd!

GROOVE RECORDS

Duo in the studio
Melody's brother, Dwayne, is a singer, too. After hearing her solo, he invites her to sing backup on his new record!

Melody's world

Melody loves spending time with her family. She goes to church and eats dinner with her grandparents every Sunday. On her birthday, they surprise her with a fancy winter coat!

Warm furry hat

Turn it up

Melody learns to feel more comfortable in front of a microphone, but she knows there are many ways to raise her voice.

Brocade coat

1960s-style microphone

Tambourine

Perfect harmony

Melody admires her grandmother's shiny upright piano. When Big Momma or Dwayne play, Melody sings along. Her dog, Bo, does too!

In This Year...

The long fight for equality leads to the Civil Rights Act, outlawing racial discrimination.

JULIE ALBRIGHT™

Small side braid

Julie is growing up in San Francisco in the 1970s. It is a time of change in the U.S. and in Julie's own life. Julie finds some changes hard to get used to, like her parents getting divorced. But she discovers that sometimes change is worth fighting for. She campaigns to save endangered animals and to make sure girls have equal opportunities at school.

Game on

Julie is all about getting in the game, whether it's on a basketball court or in an arcade. She knows the power of a positive attitude!

Bell-bottom jeans

ALL ABOUT ME

★ Favorite colors: **Purple and yellow**

★ Favorite food: **Chocolate fondue**

★ Best friends: **Ivy, T.J., and Nutmeg, her pet rabbit**

★ Best birthday celebration: **A picnic at the beach**

Julie's world

DID YOU KNOW?
Julie's nickname on the basketball court is "Cool Hand Albright" because she passes the ball so swiftly.

Julie's favorite sport is basketball. There is no girls' basketball team at school, so she petitions to be allowed to play on the boys' team.

Speakers built into chair

Mesh top with team logo

Chill-out time

After school or basketball practice, Julie relaxes in her stereo egg chair. She can turn on the tunes and put up her feet on her plush orange ottoman.

In This Year...

There is an oil shortage in America. People carpool, walk, or ride bikes to save gas.

Handmade holiday

Mom's new apartment is small, but there's always room for holiday cheer! Julie hand-makes gifts for her sister, Tracy, and Mom to open by the fire.

IVY LING™

In her bustling Chinese American family, Ivy sometimes feels invisible. Her dad works two jobs and her mother is always busy studying. On top of that, Ivy's best friend, Julie, moved to another part of San Francisco! But Ivy learns that by making her own decisions, she can make her own good luck, too.

Chandelier earrings

ALL ABOUT ME

★ Nickname: **Poison Ivy**

★ Best friend: **Julie Albright**

★ Favorite sport: **Gymnastics**

★ Favorite holiday: **Chinese New Year**

Forever friends

Ivy sees Julie whenever she comes back to the old neighborhood to stay with her dad. They have sleepovers, shoot hoops, and go shopping—just like old times!

Bag made from blue jeans

In This Year...

Crafts using recycled materials—such as an old pair of blue jeans—are popular.

Ivy's world

Ivy loves Chinese New Year traditions, from making decorations to watching the dragon parade. The holiday lasts for 15 days and includes visits with family and friends.

DID YOU KNOW?
Ivy's red silk dress is a holiday tradition—her family always buys new clothing for the new year.

Long forks for dipping

Fondue pot

Chocolate fondue
Ivy's family celebrates New Year with traditional Chinese sweets and American sweets, too. Ivy's favorite American treat is chocolate fondue.

Brocade pattern

Parade day
During Chinese New Year, colorful paper lanterns, bright banners, and popping firecrackers decorate the streets of Chinatown. Ivy thinks they look magical.

COURTNEY MOORE™

My year is 1986

Courtney loves playing video games at the mall near her home in southern California. When she gets to create her own game, she gives it a female superhero. But Courtney soon realizes that all a hero needs to bring about change is a little courage.

Crop top

DID YOU KNOW?
Courtney's mom is running to be Orange Valley's first woman mayor!

At the mall
Courtney mixes and matches clothes to come up with bright, bold outfits. She experiments to see how many outfits she can make.

Boots with scrunched tops

ALL ABOUT ME

★ Favorite color: **Purple**

★ Hobbies: **Watching music videos, renting movies, and going to the mall**

★ Pet: **A guinea pig named Parsley**

★ Role model: **Christa McAuliffe, a teacher chosen to go into space**

Courtney's world

Courtney shares a room with her stepsister, Tina. Being part of a blended family isn't always easy. But the more Courtney shares her interests, and her feelings, the closer her family becomes.

Family time

Courtney sinks into her beanbag chair to watch TV with her family. She can work out with Mom by popping a workout video into the VCR!

VCR plays video tapes

Cropped sweatshirt

Starry-eyed student

Courtney loves learning about space. She even dreams up a space-traveling superhero named Crystal Starshooter, who travels the galaxy looking for ways to save the Earth.

In This Year...

On January 28, the space shuttle Challenger *explodes shortly after launch.*

Knit leg warmers

LINDSEY BERGMAN™

My year is 2001

Beaded bobby pin

Lindsey dreams of making the world a better place, but sometimes her best intentions lead her into trouble. But when her brother goes through a tough time, Lindsey steps up and comes through.

Busy bee

Lindsey tries to play matchmaker to her teachers, find her lost dog, and stop the bullying at school. She uses her laptop and notebook to keep track of her plans.

Striped-arm hoodie

In This Year...

Laptop computers are popular, but most Americans don't yet have an Internet connection. Information is transferred on computer disks.

ALL ABOUT ME

★ Extracurricular activity: **Playing trumpet in the school band**

★ Pet: **A dog named Mr. Tiny**

★ Favorite way to get around: **Scooter**

★ Favorite animal: **Dog**

Lindsey's world

Lindsey gets from place to place on her shiny scooter. Her butterfly helmet keeps her safe while she zooms down the sidewalk.

THURSDAY
10-18-2001
A 11-30 47

Staying connected

Lindsey takes her laptop computer everywhere. She carries it in a messenger-style bag along with a notebook, pencil, and computer disks.

DID YOU KNOW?

Lindsey's idea to cover ugly trashcans with smiley face stickers backfires when she gets into trouble for damaging property!

KAILEY HOPKINS™

Sporty Kailey loves living by the sea. When a new development threatens her favorite beach and the creatures living there, Kailey works to save the shoreline. She learns that a person is never too young, or too old, to speak out for what they believe in.

Ruffled embroidered sundress

ALL ABOUT ME

★ Favorite sports: **Boogie boarding and snorkeling**

★ Pet: **Sandy the dog**

★ Favorite place: **The beach**

★ Lives in: **Southern California**

Best friends

Kailey takes her dog, Sandy, wherever she goes. Whether they are out for a walk or surfing the waves together, Sandy and Kailey always have fun.

Woven sandals

In This Year...

California's Long Beach Department of Parks, Recreation and Marine receives a gold-medal award for its public programs.

Kailey's world

Kailey spends all her free time at the beach. Her favorite thing to do is look at the tide pools. Each pool is like its own little world.

Catch a wave

Boogie-board bag

Kailey enjoys riding waves to the shore on her boogie board. It is covered in a silvery starfish design and includes a wrist leash so her board can't be swept away by the waves.

Colorblock wetsuit

Ocean fun

Kailey wears her sparkly bikini when she searches the beach's tide pools for marine creatures. She always makes sure they're safe from harm.

MARISOL LUNA™

Crocheted cap

Marisol loves to dance! So when her parents decide to move to the suburbs of Chicago, she is sad to find that her new neighborhood doesn't have a dance studio. With the help of new friends, Marisol persuades a local dancer to start teaching dance classes.

Jazzed up

Marisol enjoys lots of different types of dance, including jazz and tap. In her shimmery purple costume, Marisol is ready to perform a jazz routine.

In This Year...

The Joffrey Ballet celebrates its 10th anniversary in Chicago, after moving there from New York City in 1995.

Shiny cargo pants

ALL ABOUT ME

- ★ Pet: **Rascal the cat**
- ★ Favorite type of dance: **Ballet folklórico (Mexican folk dance)**
- ★ Motto: **"Never give up your dreams."**
- ★ School champion at: **Two-Square, a playground game**

Marisol's world

Dancing is close to Marisol's heart, but following her passion can be hard work. No matter what challenges she faces, Marisol always does her best.

Glittery top hat

Purple feather boa

Long-sleeved leotard

Performance prep
When Marisol has a dance performance, she packs her trunk with all of the supplies she needs to deliver a great show.

AMERICAN GIRL THEATER

Fringe skirt

Practice makes perfect
Marisol loves all kinds of dance. She has never taken ballet before and she finds the classes difficult at first. But she keeps practicing and improving.

DID YOU KNOW?
Marisol's neighbor Miss Mendoza, a former professional dancer, inspires and encourages Marisol to keep working at ballet.

Tap shoes

JESS McCONNELL™

Loose braids

Jess is excited to leave the United States for the first time and travel to Belize in Central America with her archaeologist parents. They spend five months at a dig of ancient Mayan ruins. In Belize, Jess discovers lots of new things about the world—and about herself.

Swing time

Jess enjoys sitting in her swinging chair with Toshi the monkey. Together, they listen to the sounds of the jungle.

Tie-dye print skirt

DID YOU KNOW?
Jess has a mix of Japanese, Scottish, and Irish ancestry.

ALL ABOUT ME

★ Home state: **Michigan**
★ Hobby: **Soccer**
★ Favorite instrument: **Guitar**
★ Foster pet: **Pippi the parrot**

Jess's world

Jess has never traveled far from home before. She is looking forward to an adventure filled with exploring, spotting new animals, and trying things she's never done, such as kayaking.

Adventure accessories

Jess can carry everything she needs in her tote bag. It's the best place to keep her passport, a map, a bottle of water, a guidebook, and her butterfly camera while she's exploring.

Belize guidebook

Long-sleeve swim top

River ready

Jess is always up for a challenge. In Belize, she paddles through river rapids in an inflatable kayak for the first time.

In This Year...

Archaeologists discover the earliest example of Mayan writing in a cave. The carefully drawn symbols are likely to be at least 2,200 years old.

Kayaking shoes

NICKI FLEMING™

Nicki loves volunteering for projects at school or on her family's ranch, especially if it means working with animals. Sometimes she takes on more than she can handle, but Nicki always finds a way to make things work.

★ ALL ABOUT ME ★

★ Favorite sport: **Skiing**

★ Favorite hobby: **Art**

★ Loves: **Animals**

★ Favorite animals: **Sprocket the puppy and Jackson the horse**

Cowgirl-style boots

DID YOU KNOW?
Nicki names her twin sisters, Rebecca and Kristine, after her best friends, Becca and Kris.

Gala girl
Nicki works hard to make her school's gala event a success. She dresses in her best outfit for the big night, pairing a pretty twill jacket with a floral mesh skirt.

Nicki's world

Nicki spends lots of time outdoors on her Colorado ranch. She especially loves riding her horse, Jackson, in the Rocky Mountains.

Horse tack box

Horse helper

On the ranch, Nicki helps to look after the horses. She grooms them and gives them treats. She stores their supplies in a blue tack box.

Mountain ride

Nicki rides Western-style, using the same type of saddle and bridle that cowboys use.

In This Year...

2007 marks 100 years since conservationists began their campaign to create Rocky Mountain National Park.

NICKI

Chaps protect Nicki's legs when she rides

MIA ST. CLAIR™

Mia loves being on the ice and dreams of one day becoming a professional figure skater. By working hard to improve her skating, Mia knows she can achieve her dream.

On display

Mia's passion for figure skating shows in her bedroom. She decorates her room with skating ribbons and trophies.

Jersey skating skirt

In This Year...

Californian figure skater Mirai Nagasu wins gold at the United States Figure Skating Championships held in Minnesota.

ALL ABOUT ME

★ Favorite activities: **Figure skating and playing hockey with her brothers**

★ Funniest moment: **Skating while dressed as a giant squirrel**

★ Coach's motto: **"Win or lose, always be a good sport."**

Mia's world

DID YOU KNOW?
To help with ice-skating costs, Mia volunteers at the Lucerne Skate Club—the rink where she practices and performs figure skating.

Mia has always played hockey with her brothers, but her passion is for figure skating. Whenever Mia is on the ice, she is practicing to perfect her spins and jumps.

Hairstyling kit

Sparkly mesh sleeves

Perfect ponytail

When it's time for Mia to perform on the ice, she uses tools from her styling kit to create a hairstyle as lovely as her skating outfit.

Hockey practice

Mia puts on her hockey jersey to shoot pucks on the ice with her three hockey-playing brothers.

White figure skates

CHRISSA MAXWELL™

Chrissa is a creative girl who moves
from Iowa to Minnesota with her family.
Starting at a new school is hard, and it's
even worse when a group of girls called the
Mean Bees makes Chrissa feel unwelcome.
But Chrissa finds the courage to stand
strong in the face of bullying.

Snow style

Chrissa's new
hometown in
Minnesota is a
great place for winter
sports. Chrissa zips
down snowy slopes
on her snow tube.

Floral-print
wrap dress

DID YOU KNOW?

For her craft projects,
Chrissa uses yarn
that her nana makes
from their pet
llamas' wool.

ALL ABOUT ME

★ Favorite sports: **Swimming and diving**

★ Pet: **Starburst, a mini llama**

★ Favorite after-school activities: **Arts
and crafts, especially sewing**

Chrissa's world

At first, Chrissa has trouble fitting in at her new school. With encouragement from her best friend back in Iowa, Chrissa joins the school's swim club. It turns out to be a great place to make new friends!

Goggles and swim cap

Knitting needles and yarn

Sewing machine

Crafty girl

Chrissa enjoys making handmade gifts for her new friends, Gwen and Sonali. Her craft studio is filled with everything she needs for her sewing and knitting projects.

In This Year...

In April 2009, the U.S. passes a bill to stop cyberbullying, which includes sending mean messages online.

Dive in

Chrissa is a strong swimmer. She loves competing in swim meets and wearing the swim club's uniform.

SONALI MATTHEWS™

Silky brown hair

When Sonali's longtime friends, Tara and Jadyn, begin to bully others, Sonali tries to find the courage to stand up and speak out. After Sonali befriends Chrissa and Gwen, the three girls take a stand together against bullying at their school.

ALL ABOUT ME

★ Favorite activities: **Diving and swimming**

★ Favorite pet: **Tofu the dog**

★ New hobby: **Knitting**

★ Nervous habit: **Twisting her hair around her finger**

In This Year...

American Girl declares May 1, 2009, to be Stop the Bullying Day. Thousands of children sign pledges to stand up to bullying.

Knit tunic

Denim capris

A picnic

This lakeside party has a purpose—Chrissa, Sonali, and Gwen discuss ways to stop bullying at school and make it a friendlier place. Their parents join the conversation, too.

GWEN THOMPSON™

Gwen's family has fallen on hard times and Gwen is being bullied at school. When Chrissa befriends shy Gwen, she comes out of her shell. With Chrissa by her side, Gwen finds her confidence—and her voice.

Stronger together

These three girls learn that when it comes to standing up to bullies, friends are stronger when they stand together.

Eyelet-lace dress

ALL ABOUT ME

★ Favorite animal: **Chrissa's pet llama, Starburst**

★ New hobby: **Swimming**

★ New job: **Assistant manager for the swim team**

Braided sandals

LANIE HOLLAND™

Dragonfly headband

Lanie loves science, wildlife, and the outdoors. She longs to explore the world outside, but the rest of her family prefers to stay indoors. After her Aunt Hannah encourages Lanie to start gardening and bird-watching, Lanie realizes that outdoor adventure can be found close to home.

Sunny slumber

When the sun is shining Lanie loves to hang out in her hammock. From here she can quietly spot birds and animals to sketch in her nature journal.

ALL ABOUT ME

★ Favorite subject: **Science**

★ Pet: **Lulu the lop-eared bunny**

★ Favorite hobbies: **Gardening and sketching**

★ Dream: **To travel around the world helping protect nature and wildlife**

★ Best friend: **Dakota**

Striped rugby dress

DID YOU KNOW?

Lanie's best friend Dakota is also a nature lover. She visits the jungles of Indonesia, helping her father rescue orangutans.

Lanie's world

Lanie loves camping! Whether pitching a tent in her own backyard or staying overnight in her aunt's camper, Lanie is always well prepared.

Sleeping bag

Knit scarf

Gear to go
With a sleeping bag, camp cup, teapot, and more, Lanie has all the supplies she needs to camp out in comfort.

In This Year...
Scientists discover a new species of bird called a Limestone Leaf Warbler in Vietnam and Laos.

Bird-watching guide

Happy camper
Lanie's aunt's camper is the perfect vehicle for an outdoor adventure. It provides a cute and cozy place to eat, sleep, and shower after a day of exploring.

KANANI AKINA™

Living on the Hawaiian island of Kaua'i, Kanani is filled with the aloha spirit. She loves to make visitors feel welcome. Kanani works at her family's business, Akina's Shave Ice and Sweet Treats. She also helps protect the Hawaiian monk seal.

Hibiscus flower clip

Painted Hawaiian necklace

★ ALL ABOUT ME ★

- ★ Best friend: **Celina**
- ★ Proudest moment: **Rescuing a baby monk seal**
- ★ Enjoys: **Greeting customers at the shave ice shop**
- ★ Pets: **Jinx the rooster, Barksee the dog, and Mochi the goat**

Cool treats

On sunny days, Kanani helps tourists and beachgoers beat the heat with tasty scoops of shave ice from her family's stand.

Muumuu, a traditional Hawaiian dress

In This Year...

The National Marine Fisheries Service proposes a new plan to help protect Hawaiian monk seals.

Kanani's world

Kanani loves to share the wonders of her island with visitors. When her cousin Rachel comes from the mainland to stay with the Akinas, Kanani takes her to a feast called a luau, where she performs in a hula show.

DID YOU KNOW?
Kanani works hard to tell people about endangered Hawaiian monk seals. She raises money for them, too.

"Aloha" greeting card

Flowery lei

Sweet send-off
Kanani fills a pretty woven gift box with lots of delicious sweet treats from her parents' store. She gives the gift to Rachel as a reminder of the island.

Hula show outfit

Catch a wave
One of Kanani's favorite sports is paddleboarding. Standing on top of her board, she can explore the ocean and sea coves, looking for monk seals.

McKenna Brooks™

Star necklace from Grandma

McKenna excels in gymnastics. As she enters fourth grade, however, balancing sports with schoolwork is a challenge. When her grades start to slip, she has to find a way to keep up. A tutor helps her realize that she can use her strengths as a gymnast to succeed in the classroom, too.

Walk in the rain

McKenna's dog, Cooper, is always ready for a walk—even in the rain! There are lots of drizzly days in Seattle, but that doesn't stop McKenna from heading outside with her pup.

In This Year...

The 2012 Olympic Games are held in London, United Kingdom. American Gabby Douglas wins gold for best all-around gymnast.

Gymnastics bag

GYMNASTICS

ALL ABOUT ME

★ Best friends: **Sierra and Josie**

★ Cutest pets: **Cooper the dog and Polka Dot the hamster**

★ Gymnastics idol: **Coach Isabelle Manning**

★ Newest hobby: **Helping at the horseback riding center**

McKenna's world

McKenna works hard to try to make the Shooting Stars competitive gymnastics team, but she has even bigger dreams. She hopes to win Olympic gold someday!

Poetry journal

Performance leotard

In the bag

McKenna keeps everything she needs in her sports bag, including a journal where she writes poetry. The journal is a gift from her tutor.

Rhythmic gymnastics wand

Balancing act

The balance beam is one of McKenna's favorite events, until a scary fall shakes her confidence. She has to find the courage to get back up again.

DID YOU KNOW?
McKenna has five-year-old twin sisters, Maisey and Mara. They want to be gymnasts, too!

SAIGE COPELAND™

Whether drawing, painting, or sketching, creative Saige expresses herself through her art. With her school art classes under threat, Saige learns how to put her creative talents to use. With help from her grandmother and friends, Saige speaks out to save the art classes.

Up, up, and away

Saige and her dad love soaring high above the mountains in a hot-air balloon. From the sky, they can see all of the beauty New Mexico has to offer.

Colorful canvas purse

DID YOU KNOW?

Saige's home of Albuquerque, New Mexico, is known as the hot-air balloon capital of the world.

ALL ABOUT ME

★ Favorite class: **Art**

★ Favorite pastime: **Horseback riding**

★ Worst fear: **Speaking in public**

★ Pet: **A dog named Sam**

★ Talent: **Painting horse portraits**

Saige's world

Whether trail riding with her grandmother or painting the beautiful landscapes of New Mexico, Saige loves the great outdoors.

Work of art

To create the perfect picture, Saige first draws in her sketch pad. Once she has a rough drawing, she sets up her easel and brushes to paint her work of art.

Paintbrush holder

Belt with cowgirl-style buckle

In This Year...

The New Mexico Museum of Art curates an exhibition telling 14,000 years of cultural history in New Mexico through art.

Ranch rider

Saige's grandmother, Mimi, has many horses on her ranch. Named after the famous artist, Picasso is Saige's favorite horse.

ISABELLE PALMER™

Nine-year-old Isabelle is a dancer attending her first year at the Anna Hart School of the Arts in Washington, DC. While she loves to perform, Isabelle's nerves sometimes get the better of her, making her worry whether ballet is really for her. Learning to believe in herself, Isabelle discovers her own way to shine.

Flutter sleeve

DID YOU KNOW?
To help perfect her turns, Isabelle likes to pretend she's skipping and spinning across water.

Practice makes perfect
Isabelle likes to add a bit of shine to her performance, even in dance class. Her wrap skirt with pink and purple sequins makes Isabelle really sparkle!

Sparkly shoes

ALL ABOUT ME

★ Nicknames: **Iz and Izzie**

★ Loves: **Ballet**

★ Hobbies: **Sewing and designing dance costumes**

★ Best friends: **Luisa and Gabriel**

Isabelle's world

Isabelle is creative in more ways than one. When she's not rehearsing and performing, Isabelle makes her own costumes. Wearing her own designs gives Isabelle a confidence boost on stage.

Ballet barre

Pink sequins

Ready to dance
When it's time to practice her pliés, Isabelle uses her ballet barre, yoga mat, and accessories to stretch and warm up.

DID YOU KNOW?
A family outing to see the waterlilies at an aquatic garden inspires Isabelle's ballet dress design.

Sparkle and shine
Isabelle and her mom make costumes for the school's Autumn Festival. Isabelle makes this bright pink performance outfit covered with eye-catching sparkles for a shimmering performance.

Floaty tulle

GRACE THOMAS™

A French beret

Grace loves to bake! She can't wait to go to Paris to visit her aunt and uncle's bakery, called a *pâtisserie*. Being away from her friends all summer is hard, but Grace brings back lots of ideas for setting up a bakery with them when she returns.

★ ALL ABOUT ME ★

★ Best friends: **Maddy and Ella**

★ Favorite accessory: **A new charm bracelet**

★ Sweetest pet: **Bonbon, the French bulldog**

★ Favorite hobby: **Baking, but it's more than a hobby—it's a business!**

Cart for tarts

A pastry cart means Grace can take her baked goods on the road, along with her favorite baking assistant: Bonbon.

Stylish ankle boots

In This Year...

TV cooking shows for kids, such as MasterChef Junior, are very popular.

Grace's world

Grace enjoys biking around Paris with her mom, especially when they stop for lunch at an outdoor café. The sights, smells, and sounds all around her inspire big ideas!

Bow-shaped earrings

Menu board

French treats

Today's special
Grace can't always pronounce the French treats on the menu, but she's willing to try them all!

DID YOU KNOW?
Grace names her own business "La Petite Pâtisserie," inspired by the *pâtisseries* she visits in Paris.

Apron-style dress

Baking buddies
Working with friends is fun, but it isn't always easy. Back home, Grace and her friends learn to combine their talents in creative ways.

LEA CLARK™

Hazel eyes

Traveling to Brazil to visit her brother is a dream come true for Lea. She's a little nervous, but armed with her travel journal and her grandma's compass necklace, she's determined to push past her fears and dive into adventure. She can't wait to see the beautiful beaches and photograph animals in the rainforest!

ALL ABOUT ME

★ Role model: **Grandma Ama**

★ Best friends: **Abby and Camila**

★ Favorite pet: **Ginger the turtle**

★ Favorite hobby: **Photography— especially after winning third place in a magazine contest!**

Canvas messenger bag

DID YOU KNOW?

Lea is one-eighth Brazilian. Her great-grandpa moved to the U.S. from Brazil when he was a boy.

Braided belt

Party dress

Lea sees many Brazilian women wearing traditional white dresses. She celebrates her trip with a white dress of her own, which will always remind Lea of her time in Brazil.

Lea's world

Lea and her brother love exploring in Brazil. At the beach they snorkel, kayak, and even watch baby sea turtles hatch. In the rainforest, they are amazed by all the wildlife they can see up close.

Under the waves

Lea's ocean kayak has a clear bottom so that she can see the fish and coral reef in the water below.

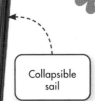

Collapsible sail

Snorkeling fins

Rainforest lullaby

Lea stays overnight in a pretty rainforest house. After a day of hiking, she relaxes in the loft bed as the sounds of the forest lull her to sleep.

In This Year...

Many people visit Brazil for the 2016 Summer Olympic Games. Ecotourism trips into the rainforest are also very popular.

GABRIELA McBRIDE™

Creative Gabriela loves performing and the arts—especially poetry. But having a stutter means expressing herself isn't always easy. Gabriela works hard to follow her passion, and learns that by speaking out she can help others, too.

Rising star

Rehearsing for her many performances takes a lot of hard work. Gabriela's stretchy practice outfit keeps her comfortable dancing for hours at a time.

Comfortable leggings

DID YOU KNOW?
Poetry is so close to Gabriela's heart that she names her cat Maya, after poet Maya Angelou.

High-top sneakers

ALL ABOUT ME

★ Nickname: **Gabby**

★ Favorite activities: **Dancing and writing poetry**

★ Proudest moment: **Performing a poem without missing a beat**

Gabriela's world

DID YOU KNOW?
Gabriela has been on stage many times, but she still gets nervous. Before each show she rubs the curtain for luck.

All of Gabriela's hard work pays off when it's time to perform. She loves putting on her costume and getting on stage.

Shoulder bag

Rehearsal essentials
Gabriela has the perfect bag for rehearsals—it's shaped like a boom box. In it she always packs water, snacks, hair accessories, and adhesive bandages.

On tape
Gabriela records rhythms for her poetry performances on an electronic drum kit. A sturdy case keeps her equipment safe.

Sequined top

Silver jazz shoes

TENNEY GRANT™

My year is 2017

Tenney plays the guitar and writes her own songs. She loves to play for others and share the music that's in her heart. Tenney dreams of making it big one day, but she is determined to stay true to herself and her music in the process.

Denim vest

DID YOU KNOW?
Tenney works at her mom's food truck. Her favorite snack is her mom's famous Nashville hot chicken.

Backstage
Before Tenney performs, she gets ready in a backstage dressing room. She feels just like the big stars she sees on stage in her hometown of Nashville, Tennessee.

Flower-decorated guitar

ALL ABOUT ME

★ Favorite activities: **Writing songs and playing music**

★ Prized possession: **Her trusty guitar**

★ Favorite songwriting spot: **In her family's backyard**

★ Pet: **Waylon, her golden retriever**

Tenney's world

It takes a lot of grit and hard work to make it as a performer. Fortunately, there's time for fun, too. When she gets together with her best friend Jaya, Tenney knows they will have a good time whatever they do.

Wide-brim hat

Southern snacks

For an afternoon in the park with her friends, Tenney packs a Southern-style picnic. Her floral picnic blanket is perfect for spreading out on the grass.

Picnic blanket with carry handle

DID YOU KNOW?
"Tenney" is short for Tennyson, after the famous British poet Alfred, Lord Tennyson.

Eyelet-lace shorts

The band

When Tenney performs, her band partner Logan plays drums. Tenney feels less nervous with Logan on stage— she knows that she can count him to keep a steady rhythm.

LOGAN EVERETT™

Fourteen-year-old Logan loves playing music with his bandmate, Tenney. Logan has to balance school and music with his responsibilities at home, and he's afraid to ask for help. When he learns to lean on Tenney, they both grow stronger—together.

ALL ABOUT ME

★ Favorite instruments: **Drums, bass, and guitar**

★ Likes: **Bike riding and Indian food**

★ Dislikes: **Flat bike tires and asking for help**

Button-down overshirt

In This Year...

Thanks to YouTube and TV talent shows, young singer-songwriters can quickly rise to fame.

In the studio

Before going on tour, Logan and Tenney record an EP, a mini album with a few songs. If their tour is a success, they'll record a full-length album!

Logan's world

When it's performance time, Logan sits down at his drums or grabs his guitar. Under the bright lights, before a crowd of cheering fans, Logan is in his happy place.

Bass drum with pedal

Brown biker jacket

Ready for rhythm

Logan's drum set has everything he needs to set the tempo—a bass drum, a snare drum, a cymbal, and a stool.

DID YOU KNOW?
Logan's dad taught him how to play guitar, but Logan taught himself how to play drums.

Outdoor stage

When they perform together Logan plays guitar and Tenney sings. They don't always agree off-stage, but when they perform, they're perfectly in tune.

Z YANG™

My year is 2017

13-year-old Z loves telling stories through her videos and sharing them with family and friends. But sometimes their feedback can make her feel a little disheartened. Z learns that to be a true filmmaker, she needs to trust her instincts and share her unique take on life.

Camera T-shirt

ALL ABOUT ME

★ Pet: **Popcorn the Dalmatian**
★ Favorite activities: **Filming and editing videos, watching movies, and eating buttery popcorn**
★ First video: **A stop-motion animation film featuring Kit Kittredge**

On the go

Z is always on the lookout for a new story to turn into a video. On her three-wheeled scooter, she can get to where she needs to be quickly.

Sparkly shoes

DID YOU KNOW?

Z earns a chance to make a documentary for a film festival. This could be her big break!

Z's world

Not only does Z have a nose for a story, she is a technology whiz, too. She can operate several different kinds of cameras and uses editing equipment with ease.

Scarf worn as a headband

Camera club

Z uses a mounted camera, a digital camcorder, and her smartphone to record the things she sees. She can transfer all of the images onto her computer for editing.

Tripod holds pretend smartphone

Comfortable checked shirt

DID YOU KNOW?
Some of Z's first videos were inspired by real girls using their American Girl dolls to create stop-motion videos.

Editing suite

Back in her bedroom, Z uses editing equipment and creative thinking to turn her video footage into finished films.

LUCIANA VEGA™

Luciana dreams of being the first girl to go to Mars. When she's chosen for Space Camp, she's over the moon! But becoming a good leader and an encouraging teammate isn't easy. She has to overcome her fears in order to make her dreams come true.

Chance of a lifetime

Luciana is thrilled when she's invited to visit the Mars habitat in the Atacama Desert!

Purse belt

In This Year...

NASA launches InSight, a robotic lander, to explore the crust and interior of Mars. It reaches Mars on November 26.

Holographic boots

ALL ABOUT ME

★ Family nicknames: **Luci and Lulu**

★ Nickname for herself: **Future First Girl on Mars**

★ Best traits: **Confidence and creativity**

★ Prized possession: **Her star necklace, given to her on her first birthday**

Luciana's world

Luciana's sights are set on Mars, but her heart is with her family—especially after her parents adopt a new baby sister from Chile.

Hair in side buns

Telescope on tripod

DID YOU KNOW?
Luciana's family is from Chile, and she speaks both English and Spanish.

T-shirt with moon and heart graphic

TO THE MOON AND BACK

Aiming for the stars

At night with her telescope, Luciana can gaze at the moon, stars, and International Space Station. She looks upward and lets her dreams soar.

A Chilean celebration

Luciana spends New Year's Eve in Chile with her entire family. She has fifteen cousins!

BLAIRE WILSON™

Blaire loves inventing recipes with ingredients grown on her family's farm. She helps her mom cook at their bed-and-breakfast. But Blaire's true creativity shines when she has to work through challenges to stay connected with friends.

★ ALL ABOUT ME ★

- ★ Nicknames: **Sprout and Mighty People Person**
- ★ Best friend: **Thea**
- ★ Favorite hobbies: **Cooking, decorating, and playing on her tablet**

In This Year...

Farm-to-table dining is a popular trend. Chefs cook using fresh herbs and vegetables grown on farms in their communities.

Bumblebee pattern

Strappy shoes

Wedding planning

When Cat, the farm's manager, gets engaged, Blaire offers to help plan the wedding. They'll hold it at Pleasant View Farm!

Blaire's world

Blaire feels right at home kneeling by her garden and digging in the dirt. She's proud of the food she grows, and eager to share it with her community.

Choker necklace

Wide-brim hat with bow

Floral pattern

Ready to dig
Before she gardens, Blaire reaches for her apron and gloves. The sun gets hot overhead, so she tops off her outfit with a wide-brimmed hat.

Farm friends
Blaire plants flowers and herbs with her animal friends nearby. She collects eggs laid by Dandy the Chicken, too!

Sturdy farm boots

JOSS KENDRICK

When it comes to surfing, Joss is all in. But when her brother dares her to try out for cheer, she finds that she likes cheer, too. Joss feels torn between two worlds, until she discovers that maybe she can do and be more than one thing.

Wave-print hoodie

ALL ABOUT ME

★ Pet: **Her bulldog, Murph**

★ Best friend: **Sofia**

★ Role model: **Pro surfer Tina Hart**

★ Proudest moments: **Mastering the frontside air and the back walkover**

In This Year...

Surfing is included in the Olympic Games for the first time, but the Games are canceled because of a pandemic.

Zigzag stitching

Beach sandals

Sharing a wave

Joss's favorite surf spot is the Break at Huntington Beach. When Murph the Surf Dog joins her, they catch waves at Dog Beach instead.

Joss's world

Joss discovers that cheerleaders are tough athletes! When she's invited to be a flyer, she has to work hard and rely on her teammates, especially during competitions.

DID YOU KNOW?

Joss was born with hearing loss. When she's not wearing her hearing aid, she uses American Sign Language.

Sparkly bow

Shine Athletics graphic

Team spirit

On competition day, matching uniforms remind Joss and her team that they're all in it together—win or lose.

Her phone shows the surf report!

Girl on the go

Joss is always running to the beach or the cheer gym, so she packs a bag with her essentials, including Surf Sister bracelets, which were a gift from Sofia.

KIRA BAILEY™

My year is 2021

When Kira's aunts invite her to their wildlife sanctuary in Australia, Kira jumps at the chance! Caring for koalas, kangaroos, wombats, and wallabies is a dream come true, but it's a big responsibility, too.

Tie-dye tank

DID YOU KNOW?

Kira fosters kittens back home in Michigan. She cares for them until they're old enough to be adopted.

Wraparound bracelet

★ ALL ABOUT ME ★

★ Nickname: **Bean—a name she gives to a baby koala, too**

★ Favorite new food: **A damper, or soda bread cooked in ashes and dipped in syrup**

★ Role model: **Aunt Mamie, a veterinarian**

Tent mates

In Australia, Kira makes a new friend, Alexis, and the girls share a tent at the bush camp. Alexis loves animals just as much as Kira does!

Kira's world

Whether Kira is helping out in the animal clinic or searching for lost animals in the sanctuary, she's always looking for ways to pitch in.

Over-the-shoulder pouch

Animal-print scrub top

Rescuing a wallaby

When a bushfire threatens the sanctuary, Kira rescues a baby wallaby. She tucks it in a pouch, where it feels safe and snug, and nurses it back to health with a bottle.

Letting go

Part of caring for animals is letting them go when they're ready. It's hard for Kira to say goodbye, but she knows her animal friends are happiest in the wild.

In This Year...

WIRES, Australia's largest wildlife rescue organization, cares for animals who have lost their homes to bushfires and droughts.

Lace-up sneakers

Chapter 2
Furry friends

Whether doting on dogs, caring for cats, or sharing their hearts with horses, girls know the importance of looking after all kinds of animals—and having fun with them, too.

STEPS HIGH

Kaya's beloved horse, Steps High, is a beautiful Appaloosa mare. Steps High chooses Kaya. When the horse sees Kaya for the first time, she nudges her head against Kaya's leg. Kaya knows from that day on that Steps High will be hers.

DID YOU KNOW?
Steps High gets her name because she "steps high," or prances, when she gets excited.

Saddle pad

Fringed blanket

Spotted Appaloosa coat

Together again
When Kaya and Steps High are reunited after her mare is captured, Kaya finds that Steps High has a foal. She names him Sparks Flying. Now Kaya has two horses to love!

ALL ABOUT ME

★ Personality: **Graceful and strong**

★ Favorite activity: **Running as fast as the wind**

★ Proudest moment: **Saving Kaya's sister Speaking Rain from the river**

PENNY

Penny is a Thoroughbred mare who is mistreated by her owner, Jiggy Nye. When Felicity Merriman first meets Penny, she decides right away to help Penny escape from her cruel owner. Thanks to Felicity, the mare gains her independence at a time when America is fighting for its own.

DID YOU KNOW?
Felicity gives Penny her name. It is short for inde-PEN-dence, and celebrates Penny's spirit.

ALL ABOUT ME

★ Personality: **Spirited**

★ Favorite treat: **Sugar**

★ Bravest moment: **Leaping a fence to freedom**

Royal blue saddle blanket

Adjustable stirrups

To the ball
By proudly pulling the carriage, Penny gets to go to the Christmas Eve ball with Felicity and her friend Elizabeth. Felicity's greatest holiday gift is having Penny by her side.

INKPOT

Caroline Abbott has loved her pet cat, Inkpot, since Papa brought him home as a tiny stray kitten. His rumbling purr comforts her when she's scared or lonely. Inkpot sticks close to Caroline when she sits by the hearth or sleeps in her bed— until the urge to chase mice strikes!

White patch on chest

Bedtime buddies

Inkpot likes to curl up in Caroline's canopy bed. When he wants to go outside, he wakes her with a gentle touch of his paw on her cheek.

DID YOU KNOW?
According to Caroline's father, sailors believe black cats are good luck!

SOMBRITA

DID YOU KNOW?
Sombrita means "little shadow." This goat follows Josefina everywhere—just like a shadow!

When Florecita the goat dies and leaves a tiny orphan behind, Josefina Montoya is determined to raise her. She names the little goat Sombrita, and gives her a silver bell so she can hear her wherever she goes. Together, they explore the hills near their home on a New Mexican rancho.

Black stripe down back

ALL ABOUT ME

★ Personality: **Frisky and playful**

★ Favorite place to be petted: **Behind the ears**

★ Favorite chores: **Fetching water and herbs with Josefina**

Silver bell

Little helper

After Josefina finds baby Sombrita and nurses her back to health, Josefina realizes she wants to be a healer like her aunt. Sombrita stays by Josefina's side when she collects healing herbs from the garden.

COCHON

Cécile Rey's colorful parrot, Cochon, has brilliant red and green feathers and a loud squawk. Cécile has to be careful what she says around him—he often repeats people's words! He even knows how to say, "Pecans, girl! Pecans!" to demand his favorite treat.

DID YOU KNOW?
Cochon means "pig" in French—which suits this hungry parrot!

In the parlor
Cochon keeps Cécile company while she reads or writes letters. When he gets too noisy, she puts a blanket over his cage to quiet him.

Metal birdcage

ALL ABOUT ME

★ Personality: **Loud, bold, and noisy**

★ Favorite snack: **Pecans**

★ Favorite place: **Cécile's shoulder**

★ Favorite activity: **Mimicking someone's words**

ARGOS

ALL ABOUT ME

★ Personality: **Friendly, loyal, and protective**

★ Breed: **Bouvier des Flandres**

★ Favorite place: **By Marie-Grace's side**

Ever since Marie-Grace Gardner was very young, her dog Argos has been her constant companion. He has huggable shaggy fur and a curly tail. His size scares some people when they first meet him, including Marie-Grace's friend, Cécile. But Cécile soon learns that this enormous dog is a little sweetheart.

Buddy guard

Whether Marie-Grace is walking to her singing lessons or heading off to the market, she's never alone. Argos walks close by to protect her, especially on busy streets.

DID YOU KNOW?

Uncle Luc rescued Argos when he was a puppy and gave him to Marie-Grace.

Shaggy gray fur

MISSY

Kirsten Larson's cat, Missy, is one of her favorite animals on the farm. When Missy has kittens, one is so tiny that its heartbeat feels like the flutter of butterfly wings. Kirsten falls in love with the little kitten. It has a gray coat and bright green eyes, just like its mother.

ALL ABOUT ME

★ Personality: **Sweet, strong, and protective**

★ Best feature: **Super-soft gray fur**

★ Favorite activity: **Keeping the barn mouse-free**

★ Favorite hangout: **A pile of straw in the warm barn**

Pink-tipped ears

Cozy quilt

Kirsten helps Missy care for her tiniest kitten. She keeps it warm in her lap while she works on her quilt. The finished quilt keeps them all cozy at bedtime, too.

Soft furry paws

DID YOU KNOW?

Only one of Missy's kittens is all gray like her. The others are black and white or gray and white.

SUNNY

Sunny, a canary, belongs to Addy Walker's new neighbor and friend, M'dear. When Sunny cocks his head and puffs out his chest, he sings a special song full of hope and happiness. Sunny's song reminds Addy to let her own spirit sing, too, even when times are hard.

DID YOU KNOW?
For Addy's birthday, M'dear gives her two of Sunny's feathers to pin in her hair.

ALL ABOUT ME

★ Personality: **Bright and cheerful**
★ Favorite activity: **Singing**
★ Favorite place: **On the perch, overlooking a room**

Wooden perch

A special bird
Addy first meets M'Dear when she goes to take a closer look at Sunny. The wise older woman soon becomes her friend. Addy loves to visit M'Dear and hear Sunny's joyful song.

JIP

Jip is a playful cocker spaniel who brings plenty of excitement to Samantha Parkington's life. Even though he sometimes leaves muddy paw prints on her pinafore, Jip's sweetness makes up for it every time.

Long, droopy ears

Pup at the party

Jip meets Samantha when Uncle Gard and Aunt Cornelia bring him to her birthday party. Even though Jip runs off with Samantha's new teddy bear, Samantha can't help but love him anyway.

ALL ABOUT ME

★ Personality: **Frisky, playful, and mischievous**

★ Eye color: **Brown**

★ Favorite activities: **Swimming and playing with Samantha**

★ Favorite hangout: **Grammercy Park**

Soft, silky fur

REBECCA'S KITTENS

When a neighbor's cat goes missing, Rebecca Rubin finds the sneaky feline in the basement of her apartment building—along with two baby kittens! Rebecca cares for them while their owner, Mr. Rossi, recovers from a winter cold.

ALL ABOUT US

★ Personality: **Cuddly and playful**
★ Favorite activity: **Snuggling with their mother**
★ Special treat: **Warm milk**
★ Home: **The basement of Rebecca's apartment building**

Not so sleepy

The kittens have a sleepover at Rebecca's. They play with the tassels on her pillow before curling up to sleep.

DID YOU KNOW?

The kittens' mother's name is Pasta because she prefers to eat spaghetti rather than mice.

Amber-rimmed eyes

GRACE

During the Great Depression when many people are out of work, Grace the basset hound is abandoned by an owner who can't afford to feed her. Luckily, Kit Kittredge finds the hungry hound and brings her home.

ALL ABOUT ME

★ Personality: **Lazy but lovable**

★ Favorite activity: **Chasing chickens— or just sleeping outside their coop**

★ Best friend: **Kit**

Adorable freckles

Droopy ears and eyes

DID YOU KNOW?
This basset hound is so clumsy that Kit's aunt Millie jokes that there is only one name for her: Grace!

Special delivery

When Kit delivers eggs in her neighborhood, Grace goes along for the ride. There's a special place for Grace to sit in Kit's homemade scooter.

MELE

Nanea's dog Mele is a "poi dog," a Hawaiian phrase for a mixed-breed dog. She's energetic and smart—so smart that she learns how to dance the hula! When Nanea brings Mele to visit injured soldiers in hospitals, she boosts their spirits with her sweet, silly personality.

Hula dog

When Nanea performs at the USO for soldiers, Mele is right there beside her. She can stand on her hind legs, trot forward and back, and do a twirl.

ALL ABOUT ME

★ Nicknames: **Silly dog and hula dog**
★ Favorite foods: **Fish and sausage**
★ Least favorite thing: **Air-raid sirens**

Soft gray fur

BENNETT & YANK

These Jack Russell terriers belong to Molly McIntire and her friend Emily Bennett, who comes to stay with the McIntires to escape bombing in London during World War II.

A puppy party

Bennett and Yank are the biggest and best surprises on Molly's tenth birthday. They join Molly and Emily for an English teatime birthday party.

Molly's puppy Bennett

Emily's puppy Yank

ALL ABOUT US

★ Personalities: **Smart, athletic, and mischievous**

★ Favorite activities: **Performing tricks and playing fetch and tug-of-war**

★ Favorite things to chew: **Paper dolls, pillows, and schoolbooks**

SCOOTER

A lovable old dachshund, Scooter is Maryellen Larkin's constant companion. With his short legs and roly-poly body, he waddles more than he walks! He co-stars in her made-up television shows, but he makes an even better audience. He settles right into the nearest comfortable spot, and then he's all ears.

ALL ABOUT ME

★ Personality: **Sleepy, sweet, and sometimes stubborn**

★ Favorite activity: **Napping**

★ Favorite hangout: **The closest shady place**

DID YOU KNOW?
Dachshunds have a loud voice—and they enjoy using it. Scooter barks along with children, train whistles, and even the doorbell.

Soft tan fur

Bedtime buddies
At nighttime, Scooter climbs into bed with Maryellen. He might snore a little, but he knows she won't mind.

Pretty patterned collar

Bo

Like his owner, Melody Ellison, this terrier has an ear for music. When he howls along to songs, Bo has perfect pitch. He's perfectly behaved when he goes on visits with Melody. He wags his tail politely but doesn't bark—unless someone plays music. Then he has to join in!

Soft, fluffy ears

DID YOU KNOW?
Bo was named "Bojangles" after the tap dancer Bill "Bojangles" Robinson. Bo doesn't dance, but he sure can sing!

Collar and leash

Bark for the park
When Bo and Melody walk past a neglected park, he inspires Melody to fix it up. He barks as if to say, "Do something!" and Melody listens.

NUTMEG

Nutmeg is Julie Albright's lop-eared bunny.
Julie's mom's new apartment doesn't allow
pets, so Nutmeg lives at Julie's dad's house.
Julie gives Nutmeg extra love and
attention when she stays with her dad.

DID YOU KNOW?
Rabbits can learn
to respond to their
names as well as to
simple commands
such as "Come!"

Floppy ears

ALL ABOUT ME

★ Personality: **Calm and snuggly**
★ Favorite activity: **Cuddling in Julie's lap**
★ Favorite foods: **Crisp carrots and apple peels**
★ Favorite hangout: **The laundry basket or the hutch in the backyard**

Wicker basket

Bunny in a basket

Nutmeg snuggles with Julie before bed
each night, but she has her own basket
for sleeping in. With its high sides,
Nutmeg feels safe and snug.

PARSLEY

Courtney loves her guinea pig, Parsley, because he was a gift from her dad. When he comes to live with Courtney at her mom's, he helps her miss Dad less. But Courtney's stepsister, Tina, isn't a big fan of Parsley! He has to work hard to win her over.

DID YOU KNOW?
Courtney has to clean Parsley's cage three times a week so that Tina won't complain about the smell, but he's worth it!

ALL ABOUT ME

★ Personality: **Sweet and curious**
★ Favorite foods: **Carrots, cucumber, and parsley (of course!)**
★ Favorite activities: **Obstacle courses and playing with ping-pong balls**

Hanging out

Courtney keeps Parsley in the bedroom she shares with Tina. She lets him out of his cage often so that they can play or listen to music together.

White and caramel-colored fur

SANDY

Sandy is a golden retriever who lives in California with her owner, Kailey Hopkins. A true beach dog, Sandy enjoys the sand and surf almost as much as Kailey does. If Kailey splashes into the ocean, Sandy is sure to dive in, too.

ALL ABOUT ME

★ Personality: **Playful, curious, and athletic**

★ Favorite activity: **Chasing waves and digging holes in the sand**

★ Favorite hangout: **In the surf or snoozing on a beach towel**

DID YOU KNOW?
Golden retrievers have coats that repel water. No wonder Sandy can play in the ocean for hours and never get cold.

Lavender bandanna

Beach buddy
While Kailey snorkels or boogie boards, Sandy takes a swim— or a roll in the sand.

Strong legs for swimming

RASCAL

DID YOU KNOW?
Himalayan cats need daily brushing. Rascal doesn't like being brushed, so Marisol has to work hard to get the job done.

A fluffy Himalayan cat, Rascal showed up on Marisol Luna's doorstep one rainy night. Ever since then, he's been her best friend— making her laugh with his antics and making her worry when he wanders away and doesn't come straight back home. He prances instead of walks and is full of personality.

ALL ABOUT ME

★ Personality: **Lazy by day, active by night**
★ Favorite activities: **Climbing, chasing birds, and watching Marisol dance**
★ Favorite hangouts: **Curled up inside Marisol's dance bag**

Bright blue eyes

Out for a stroll

Rascal loves being outside. When Marisol heads to dance lessons, he tags along for a while—until he spots a bird to watch.

SPROCKET

A service dog in training, Sprocket tries to listen to his trainer, Nicki Fleming. But he's still young and still learning, so he sometimes makes mistakes. No one knows his breed. Australian shepherd? Border collie? Bernese mountain dog? Maybe all of the above! But one thing is certain: Nicki adores him.

DID YOU KNOW?
Sprocket, like many service dogs, comes from a shelter. He has an important job to do, but he gets a forever home, too.

Plenty of pockets
When he's out and about, Sprocket wears his service-dog vest. It has lots of pockets so he can carry things for his owner. Nicki keeps his treats in there, too.

ALL ABOUT ME

★ Personality: **Smart, curious, and sweet**

★ Favorite activity: **Going on long walks**

★ Favorite hangout: **On Nicki's bed, as a special treat**

Collar with an "S" tag

JACKSON

ALL ABOUT ME

★ Personality: **Sweet, steady, and strong**

★ Favorite activities: **Going for a gallop and being groomed**

★ Favorite snacks: **Apples, carrots, and oats**

★ Favorite place: **A mountain meadow in the spring**

A handsome buckskin horse, Jackson lives on a Colorado ranch with his owner, Nicki Fleming. Her family keeps lots of horses. But since Jackson belongs to Nicki, he gets special treatment. In return, he's a steady friend who helps her cope with her changing family and friendships.

Western-style saddle

Removable bridle

DID YOU KNOW?
"Buckskin" is a color of horse, not a breed. Nicki thinks Jackson's golden coat is gorgeous, especially in sunlight.

Out for a walk

Jackson loves walking through the woods and fields just as much as Nicki does. Up in the saddle, Nicki feels as though she can see for miles.

STARBURST

Named for the way she "bursts" into Chrissa Maxwell's life one summer morning, Starburst is a mini llama. She's a special gift from Chrissa's grandmother, who has two llamas—Cosmos and Checkers. Starburst is just a little baby, but she's big on personality!

DID YOU KNOW?

Crias, or baby llamas, can walk within a few hours of being born. Chrissa is lucky enough to see Starburst take her first steps.

Woven halter and lead

ALL ABOUT ME

★ Personality: **Curious, mischievous, sweet, and energetic**

★ Favorite activity: **Exploring the world outside**

★ Favorite place: **Nestled beside her momma, Cosmos**

Fleece blanket with pockets

Guest of honor

When Chrissa and her parents throw a party at their house, who bursts onto the scene, ready to play? It's Starburst, of course!

121

LULU

A pet rabbit who loves to be outdoors, Lulu enjoys sunning on the deck or taking walks around the neighborhood with her owner, Lanie Holland. When Lanie clips a leash onto Lulu's walking vest, Lulu jumps for joy. Lulu leads the way outside, stopping to sniff the plants—or sometimes to chase the neighbor's cat!

ALL ABOUT ME

★ Personality: **Curious and friendly**

★ Favorite treats: **Fresh grass, vegetables, and alfalfa pellets**

★ Favorite hideout: **The crook of Lanie's elbow**

DID YOU KNOW?
Some rabbit owners take classes on leash-training their rabbits. Lanie teaches Lulu herself, first getting her used to the leash indoors.

Orange leash

Fun outdoors
Lanie takes Lulu for walks around the bedroom before heading outside. When Lulu does a happy leap in the backyard, Lanie knows Lulu loves to be outdoors as much as she does.

122

LANIE'S WILD ANIMALS

When Lanie goes hiking or camping, she keeps an eye out for wild animals. Will she spot a red fox, a gray squirrel with a bushy tail, a ring-tailed raccoon, or a snowy owl? Thanks to the wildflower garden she plants, she sees plenty of Monarch butterflies—right in her own backyard.

DID YOU KNOW?
Monarch butterflies lay their eggs on milkweed. Lanie plants it to invite monarchs into her garden.

Looking up

Lying in her hammock, Lanie looks out for wildlife. To remember what she sees, she records everything in her nature journal.

Raccoon

Snowy owl

Red fox

Gray squirrel

BARKSEE

This friendly tan-and-white mutt lives with his owner, Kanani Akina, on the Hawaiian island of Kaua'i. Although his name has the word "bark" in it, he only barks to alert Kanani to unusual sounds and sights—like the baby monk seal stranded on the beach who needs their help.

DID YOU KNOW?

Kanani's family rescued Barksee from an animal shelter. He was scrawny and scared, but they helped him become healthy and happy again.

ALL ABOUT ME

★ Personality: **Sweet and friendly**

★ Favorite activities: **Going for walks and barking at birds**

★ Least favorite activity: **Taking a bath**

★ Best friends: **Jinx, the rooster, and Mochi, the goat**

Warm brown eyes

A private paradise

Barksee loves running along the beach with Kanani during their afternoon walks. Sometimes they have the whole beach to themselves.

COOPER

DID YOU KNOW?
All puppies need something to chew. When McKenna runs out of puppy chews, Cooper chews her gymnastics grips instead.

A young goldendoodle, Cooper has the caramel-colored hair of a golden retriever and the curls of a poodle. He has as much energy as his owner, McKenna Brooks. So when she injures herself doing gymnastics, he knows how hard it is for her to rest. He stays by her side until she heals.

Under the bed

Some dogs love hanging out on beds. Cooper's favorite place is underneath McKenna's loft bed, where he keeps her company while she reads or does homework.

ALL ABOUT ME

★ Personality: **Loveable and loyal**

★ Smallest friend: **McKenna's hamster, Polka Dot**

★ Favorite activity: **Going for walks and chasing squirrels**

Curly caramel-colored fur

PICASSO

ALL ABOUT ME

★ Personality: **Noble, protective, wise, and kind**

★ Age: **Twenty-seven**

★ Favorite place to be scratched: **Just behind the ears**

★ Favorite activities: **Performing in rodeos and parades**

Picasso the horse belongs to Saige Copeland's grandma, Mimi, but he has a special bond with Saige. She has ridden him since she was small and he is always gentle with her. So when Mimi asks Saige to ride Picasso and lead an upcoming parade, she says, "yes!"

Colorful saddle blanket

Bridle with silver decoration

DID YOU KNOW?
Picasso is a Spanish Barb horse, a rare breed brought to America by Spanish soldiers and explorers in the 1500s.

A shared view

Saige thinks New Mexico looks even more beautiful when she explores it on horseback with Picasso. Sometimes Mimi saddles up another horse and rides with them.

SAM

Saige's dog, Sam, is a shaggy border collie mix. He helps Saige make friends with her new neighbor, Gabi. Sam gets along with everyone—except his brother, Rembrandt, who lives with Saige's grandma, Mimi.

DID YOU KNOW?
Sam is named after Sam Savitt, an artist who is famous for his horse illustrations.

Shaggy fur

Leash

Outdoor adventures

Going for walks is one of Sam's favorite things to do. Saige takes him out every morning and evening and sometimes on special trips for picnics.

★ ALL ABOUT ME ★

★ Personality: **Friendly and full of energy**

★ Secret talent: **Jumping fences**

★ Favorite meal: **Breakfast, because Saige shares her toast**

★ Favorite painting: **The one Saige painted of him**

TUTU

Isabelle Palmer's kitten got her name because she's as fluffy as a tutu. This diva can leap through the air as high as any ballerina—especially if there's a ribbon dangling overhead. She's also very good at keeping Isabelle and her sister, Jade, on their toes with her antics.

Sew tempting
Tutu dreams of having Isabelle's sewing room to herself. From long ribbons to measuring tape, there are so many things for a kitten to play with.

Sparkly personalized collar

DID YOU KNOW?
Tutu was a gift for Isabelle's mother, but she prefers to sleep with Isabelle and her sister, Jade.

BONBON

This French bulldog is living on the streets of Paris, France, when Grace Thomas finds her. Grace calls the pup "Bonbon" because, like the French treat, she's a little rough on the outside, but as sweet as chocolate on the inside. When Bonbon wags her tail, Grace knows the name will stick!

DID YOU KNOW?
Grace's cousin, Sylvie, calls Bonbon *petite chienne* [puh-teet shee-an], which means "little dog" in French.

ALL ABOUT ME

★ Personality: **Street-smart, playful, and super sweet**

★ Favorite activities: **Chasing cats**

★ Favorite hangout: **Outside the *pâtisserie* door**

"Pirate's patch" of black fur

Red collar and leash

Puppy training
Bonbon has to learn how to walk on a leash. When she strains at it, Grace makes her walk nicely, by Grace's side. Then Bonbon gets a treat.

ORION

Orion, a robotic dog, is the mascot at Space Camp. He barks to tell Luciana when it's time to meet the rest of Team Odyssey and to train for her first mission. With his bright eyes and wagging tail, he seems so real! Luciana wishes she could design a robot like him.

ALL ABOUT ME

★ Favorite activity: **Barking**

★ Secret feature: **A touch sensor in his back that calms him down**

★ Nap trick: **When someone pats his back three times, he falls asleep**

Magnetic mouth holds toy wrench

A girl's best friend

When Luciana and her team design a robot for a robotics competition, Orion serves as sweet inspiration.

DID YOU KNOW?
Orion was designed by Mallory, one of the Space Camp crew trainers.

Rolling wheels for feet

PENELOPE

Blaire is thrilled to adopt Penelope, a baby lamb, from a neighboring farm. Penelope is so little, Blaire has to feed her formula from a bottle! As the lamb grows, she and Blaire become fast friends. Penelope stars in cute photos and videos that Blaire posts on the farm's website.

DID YOU KNOW?
Penelope was named after Blaire's favorite DIY craft video blogger.

Soft, curly fur

Ribbon collar with flowers

Fun on the farm

Penny requires lots of care, but she brings joy and laughter, too. The sweet, curious little lamb is up for anything, including dance parties!

ALL ABOUT ME

★ Nickname: **Penny**

★ Best friend: **A goat named Dash**

★ Favorite activity: **Skidding down a plastic toddler slide**

DANDELION

Dandelion is Blaire's favorite chicken. She got her name because Blaire thinks her fluffy head looks like the dandelion puffs that grow along the fence. Dandelion is curious and brave. When Blaire accidentally leaves the coop open, the chicken heads out to explore the farm!

ALL ABOUT ME

★ Nickname: **Dandy**

★ Friendliest feature: **She's a great listener. She cocks her head and tunes in when Blaire talks**

★ Best day ever: **Serving as a junior bride at a wedding with a tiny veil!**

Silky white "feathers"

Nesting nearby

Dandy keeps Blaire company while she's gardening. In exchange, Blaire cleans Dandy's nesting box so the chicken will have a cozy place to lay her eggs.

DID YOU KNOW?
Dandy calls to Blaire with a low-pitched cluck cluck cluck called a "contentment call." It means she's happy to see Blaire!

MURPH

Joss's English bulldog, Murph, is a natural at surfing and skateboarding. She's not a very good swimmer, though, so Murph wears a life vest in the water. When she's not on a board, she's curled up near Joss for cuddles and quiet time.

DID YOU KNOW?
Murph is goofy-footed like Joss. When she skateboards, she pushes with her left paw and puts her right paw on the board.

Life jacket for safety

Surf and sand
Murph surfs with Joss and her brothers at Dog Beach. It's the only beach in Huntington Beach where dogs are allowed.

ALL ABOUT ME

★ Nickname: **Murph the Surf Dog**

★ Favorite activities: **Surfing, skateboarding, and playing tug-of-war**

★ Proudest moment: **Learning how to skateboard on a ramp**

KIRA'S ANIMAL FRIENDS

When Kira visits her aunts' wildlife sanctuary in Australia, she is surrounded by furry friends. She bottle-feeds a baby kangaroo named Blossom and a baby koala, whom she names "Bean." All the animals need her loving care so that they can one day be returned to the wild.

Koala

DID YOU KNOW?
Kira's aunts let animals back into the wild using a "soft release." They open the cage so the animals can leave when they feel ready.

Wombat

On the loose
When the wombats escape their pen, Kira worries they'll get lost or hurt. Luckily, her new friend Alex is an expert wombat wrangler!

★ ALL ABOUT US ★

★ Baby names: Baby kangaroos, koalas, and wombats are all called "joeys"

★ Favorite treats: Carrots, squash, apples, lettuce, and eucalyptus leaves

Kangaroo

Pouch safely holds a joey

Large furry paws

Long tail

Out and about

The sanctuary is bursting with animals, young and old. Kira meets an adult koala named "Mum" and watches kangaroos nibbling on grass. The sanctuary has wallabies and emus, too!

Chapter 3
Amazing places

Where do American Girl characters find inspiration? Anywhere! In a tree house in the backyard or a rainforest house in Brazil. Onstage, in the spotlight, or at home, in a cozy bedroom. No place is too big or too small.

KAYA'S TEPEE

Kaya and her family travel with the seasons to gather food, so their tepees are designed to be easily packed up and moved. Poles form the frame of the tepee and are covered with hides and tule mats. Inside, Kaya sleeps on a soft bedroll and furry pillow. When it's cold, she wraps up in warm furs and hides.

Tepee pole

Stepping outside

Kaya enjoys sleeping in her tepee, but she likes being outside best—that's where her horses are. She looks forward to greeting Steps High and Sparks Flying every morning.

Bed roll

Tule mat covering

FELICITY'S STABLES

Felicity loves visiting the stables to see Penny and her foal, Patriot. Felicity feeds and brushes the horses and cleans the stables with the help of her wheelbarrow. The horses are a lot of work, but Felicity loves spending time with them.

Penny

Patriot

Shovel

Wheelbarrow with feed bags

Cute and cozy
Felicity's friend Elizabeth often visits the stables. Together they help Patriot stay warm by dressing him in a cozy plaid coat.

CAROLINE'S PARLOR

DID YOU KNOW?
The parlor is where the Abbotts celebrate Christmas. The family gathers around the fireplace to exchange gifts.

Caroline often spends her winter afternoons sitting in the parlor with her needlework. From here, she can gaze out of the window at Lake Ontario and watch the ships coming and going. The fireplace means the room is always warm during the cold winter months.

Nautical painting

Lacy curtains

Storage drawers

Fire screen

A parlor party

During the War of 1812, Caroline is lucky that her family can still celebrate special occasions. They lay out their finest treats and table settings for the parties.

JOSEFINA'S WRITING DESK

Josefina's aunt brings this elegant desk all the way from Mexico City. Designed to be portable, it looks like a plain chest on the outside, but it's beautifully decorated on the inside. Josefina can store her notebook and writing supplies in the small drawers and compartments.

Decorated lid lifts up

Drawers to hold small items

Wooden stand

Remembering Mamá

Josefina can't wait until she can read the *cuaderno*, a leather notebook filled with her mother's favorite poems and sayings. This special notebook was created by Tía Dolores.

CÉCILE'S COURTYARD

Cécile spends summer days in the garden and courtyard of her New Orleans home. She plays tag with her young cousin and then rests in the hammock between the lemon trees. When Marie-Grace visits, Cécile lays out tasty treats for them on her pretty courtyard table.

Elaborate scrollwork

Matching table

Keeping cool
Cécile and Marie-Grace keep cool in the courtyard. For extra shade, Marie-Grace pops open her fashionable lace parasol.

KIRSTEN'S BED

Pioneer children rarely had their own bedrooms, but Kirsten has a cozy nook that's all her own. Her prettily painted wooden bed provides a soft place to play with Missy and her kittens, and her washstand has a little drawer that's perfect for storing her treasures.

DID YOU KNOW?
Early settlers didn't have closets in their cabins. Instead, they kept their clothes in wooden trunks.

Hair tied in neat braids

Warm and snug
Kirsten's cabin can get very cold on winter nights. Dressed in a full-length flannel nightgown and tucked under her warm quilt, Kirsten stays toasty and snug.

Kirsten's washstand

Warm stockings

SAMANTHA'S ICE CREAM PARLOR

Samantha is excited to visit Tyson's Ice Cream Parlor in New York City. Her aunt and uncle take her there as a special treat. There are so many delicious sweets to choose from, Samantha doesn't know how she will decide which one to have!

Cash register

Pretty in pink

From the pink countertops to the gleaming soda fountain, the parlor is as pretty as Samantha had imagined. She wears her favorite dress especially for the occasion.

Pretty ice cream bowls

Soda glasses

Ornate chair

DID YOU KNOW?
Samantha's favorite ice cream flavor is peppermint.

Candy jar

TYSON'S
ICE CREAM
PARLOR

Ice cream containers

REBECCA'S MOVIE SET

Rebecca dreams of being an actress. Whether she's visiting a movie set with her cousin Max or dressing up and acting at home, she's happiest when she's performing. Rebecca's costume chest and collection of props are all she needs for inspiration.

DID YOU KNOW?
When a real-life director spots Rebecca on set, he gives her a small part in the movie they're making.

Costume chest

Pages from a script

Butterfly Queen
In her school play, Rebecca flits gracefully across the stage in her role as the Butterfly Queen. Her brocade dress has a train in the back that unfolds into butterfly wings.

KIT'S TREE HOUSE

Kit's father builds her tree house using scraps of material. At first, Kit thinks it looks a bit plain, but she uses her imagination to spruce it up. Kit loves being in her tree house, writing stories for her newspaper or playing with her friend, Ruthie.

Beaded chandelier

TREE HOUSE CLUB
MEMBERS ONLY!

Going up
Grace the dog doesn't want to miss the fun, so Kit and Ruthie let her hitch a ride in the rope and bucket "elevator."

Rope and bucket "elevator"

NANEA'S FAMILY MARKET

Nanea enjoys helping out at her grandparents' Hawaiian market. She dusts shelves filled with colorful goods and souvenirs. Nanea helps customers carry their shopping bags, too. She's proud to be able to help out, especially during wartime.

Keeping count

Because of the war, food is being rationed. Nanea's grandparents worry they'll run out of certain things, so Nanea helps them take inventory, or count what they have.

Postcard display rack

Cash register with drawer

2¢ EACH

Extra postcards

148

Red shop canopy

PONO'S MARKET

Hairslide

SPAM
SPAM SPAM
SPAM SPAM SPAM

Hawaiian
Hawaiian
Hawaiian MACADAMIA
Hawaiian
SLICED
PINEAPPLE
Hawaiian
SLICED
PINEAPPLE
Hawaiian
SLICED
PINEAPPLE

40¢

SALE!
SOUVENIR
ITEMS

$1

5¢ EACH
25¢ 3¢ 45¢
EACH
15¢ 31¢

Flower leis

Shoe stand

NANEA'S SHAVE ICE STAND

Nanea and her friends Lily and Donna can't wait to stop at the Kapahulu Corner Store for a refreshing Hawaiian treat: shave ice. The ice crystals are scooped into paper cones and topped with sweet syrup in different flavors.

Stand sign

KAPAHULU
CORNER STORE

Flavor syrups

A beach treat
Nanea enjoys shave ice at the beach, too—especially after a few hours in the sun. She and her friends build sand castles, swim, and watch surfers ride the waves.

FLAVORS

Lemon
Orange
Lime
Fruit Punch

DID YOU KNOW?
Nanea, Lily, and Donna call themselves the Three Kittens. When they mix shave ice flavors, they call it "kitten shave ice."

Menu board

MOLLY'S STAGE

Molly can't believe she has been chosen to perform as Miss Victory in her dance school's "Hooray for the U.S.A." show. The show is close to Molly's heart because it will raise money to help the war effort. Molly dances in the show while thinking of her father taking care of soldiers overseas.

DID YOU KNOW?
During the show, Molly stays calm by imagining her dad in the front row, cheering her on.

Colored stage lights

Theater curtains

Movie time
Molly loves watching movies on the big screen. She chooses her favorite snack to eat while she waits for the film to start.

Pullout stairs

MARYELLEN'S SEASIDE DINER

Maryellen looks forward to going to the Seaside Diner with her friends after school. Sometimes she shares a booth with her sister, Joan, and Joan's boyfriend, Jerry. Maryellen especially loves the burgers and shakes. When the bell dings, their order is up!

DID YOU KNOW?
Maryellen's favorite seat is one of the counter stools. She likes to watch the cooks whip up the diners' meals.

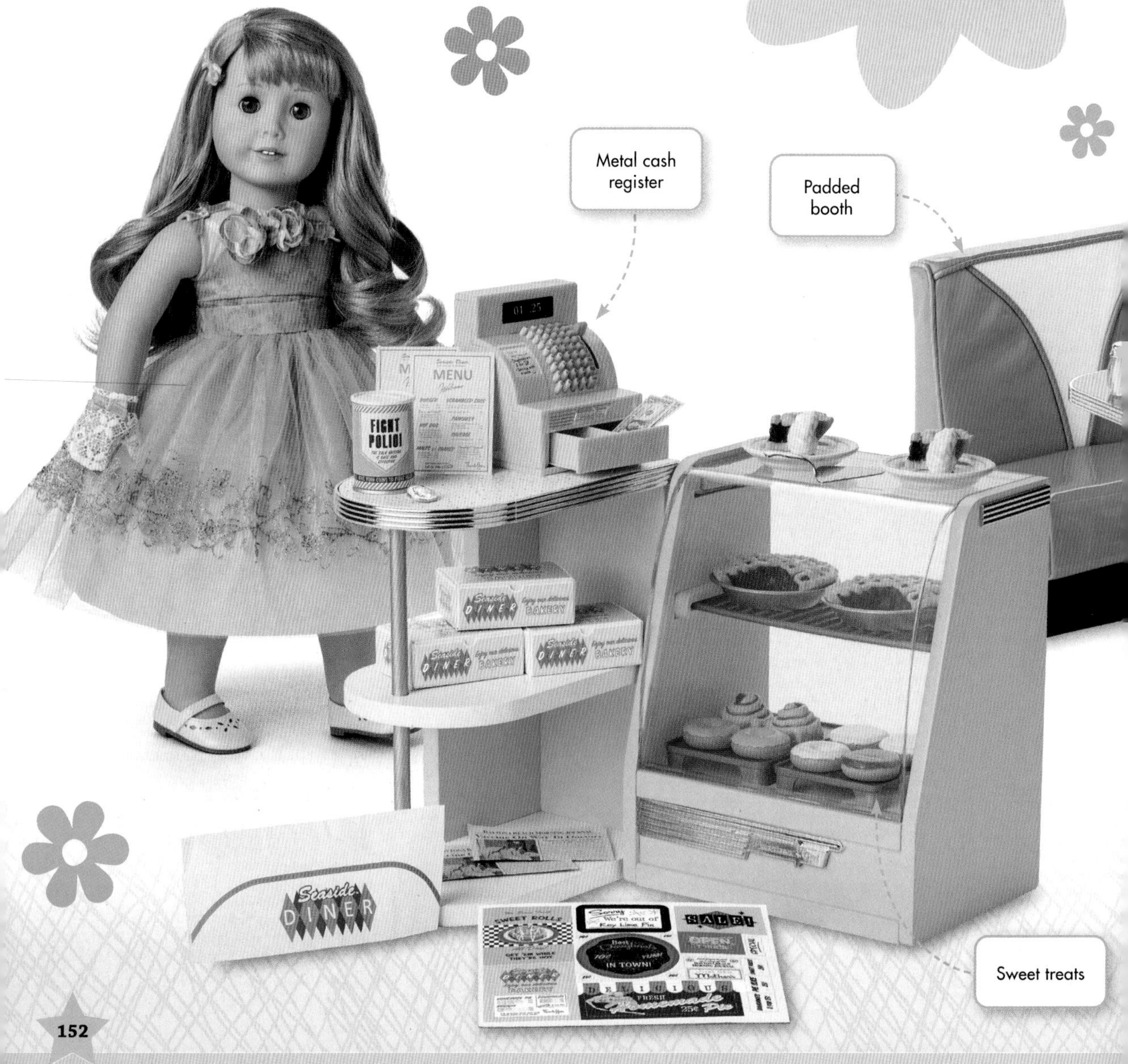

Metal cash register

Padded booth

Sweet treats

Order slips for cook

Service bell

Striped apron

Counter stools

Rock and roll

At the jukebox, Maryellen can flip through songs, push a button to choose her favorite, and then pop in a nickel to hear it play.

MELODY'S STUDIO

When Melody's brother, Dwayne, gets the opportunity to record a song, he asks Melody to sing backup. Melody is thrilled to visit a real recording studio, but she is also a little nervous. With help from her brother, Melody overcomes her nerves and sings from the heart.

Music reels

Making music

In the recording booth, Melody puts on a pair of headphones so that she can hear the background music. She then sings her part into a microphone.

DID YOU KNOW?
Melody comes up with the name for her brother's singing group, The Three Ravens.

Adjustable music stand

Headphones

JULIE'S BEDROOM

DID YOU KNOW?
Julie's mom owns a shop called Gladrags that sells homemade items like jewelry, purses, lampshades, and rugs.

For Julie, moving to a new apartment with her mom and sister means a brand-new bedroom to decorate. Julie chooses a four-poster bed with brightly colored bedding and funky beaded curtains.

Four-poster bed with canopy

Beaded curtains

Floral bedspread

In her room

Julie loves spending time in the room that she helped decorate. Sitting in her egg chair, she can call her friends, listen to music, enjoy snacks, or just kick back and relax.

JULIE'S BATHROOM

Julie adores the groovy bathroom in her family's new apartment, which her mom decorated '70s-style. She has to share it with her big sister, Tracy, so Julie always tries to wake up before Tracy so she can hop in the shower first!

Hairdryer with attachments

Flower power

After a basketball game, Julie heads to the bathroom for a hot shower. Whether she won or lost, the cheerful colors and floral patterns perk her right up.

DID YOU KNOW?
Julie's apartment is right above Gladrags, her mother's store—where Mom sells all sorts of handmade goods.

Toilet with fuzzy seat cover

Shower curtain with hooks

Head wrap

Orange-framed mirror

Butterfly wastebasket

Daisy-patterned hamper

MARISOL'S STAGE

Marisol loves nothing more than dancing! When she moves to a new neighborhood with no dance studio, Marisol persuades a local dancer to begin teaching classes. Marisol won't let anything stand in the way of her dream to become a real dancer.

In the spotlight

When Marisol has the opportunity to perform on stage, she jumps at the chance. In her rhinestone tiara and sparkly tutu, Marisol really shines.

Spinning stage

Pink spotlights

JESS'S TREE SWING

Palm tree

When Jess and her parents travel to Belize to study ancient Mayan ruins, Jess can't wait to hike, kayak, and explore. At the end of each day, she sits in her swinging chair, listens to the sounds of the jungle, and plans the next day's adventure.

DID YOU KNOW?

Jess stays in Belize for five months. She's home-schooled so she doesn't fall behind with her studies.

Swinging chair

Under the stars

At night, Jess curls up in her chair with her beloved stuffed monkey, Toshi. She writes in her journal or reads letters from her brother and sister back home.

Woven throw blanket

CHRISSA'S CRAFT STUDIO

Every crafty girl needs a place to get creative. When Chrissa comes to live with her grandmother, she creates a space for Chrissa to work. In the studio, Chrissa can sketch out her ideas and then bring them to life with yarn, needles, and thread.

DID YOU KNOW?
Chrissa's father made the bowl that holds her yarn and knitting needles.

Sketchbook for project ideas

Space for storing supplies

Craft chat

After a busy day at school, Chrissa likes to come home and work on her crafts with her grandmother. She finds it helps her to relax, and it's a good time to talk about any problems at school.

CHRISSA'S PICNIC TABLE

Chrissa's friends Sonali and Gwen love joining her after school for a picnic by the lake. The girls fill the table with plenty of delicious snacks and drinks and discuss their day at school. When the girls decide to take a stand against bullying, it's the perfect place to gather other friends from school, too.

Hanging lanterns

Polka-dot glasses

Spinning pinwheels

Table talkers

Chrissa puts out a box of table talkers— cards printed with inspirational sayings—to help get the conversation started.

Table talkers

LANIE'S HAMMOCK

While her family prefers staying indoors, Lanie satisfies her adventurous outdoor spirit in her own backyard. When she's not learning about wildlife, spotting local birds, or tending to the wildflower garden she planted, she hangs out in her hammock and writes in her nature journal.

Sunburst pattern

Hammock stand

Comfy sandals

Animal spotting

Lanie enjoys bird-watching and is always on the lookout for new species. She loves to spot wildlife on the ground, too, such as the red fox and gray squirrel.

KANANI'S SHAVE ICE STAND

Living on the Hawaiian island of Kaua'i, Kanani is always ready to spread the "aloha spirit" of welcome and friendship. She enjoys meeting people and looks forward to summer when she can help out at her family's shave ice stand.

DID YOU KNOW?
Kanani is featured in *The Daily Breeze*, the local island newspaper, after rescuing a seal.

Straw roof

PICK UP HERE

ORDER HERE

Shave ice machine

ALOHA

Save the seals

While at the beach, Kanani spots a baby monk seal trapped in a net and helps rescue it. To help save the local monk seals, Kanani raises money and public awareness at the shave ice stand.

SAVE THE MONK SEALS!

FLAVORS OF THE DAY

MANGO ✦ MANDARIN ORANGE ✦ WATERMELON ✦ STRAWBERRY ✦ COCONUT
see our menu for more!

"Save the seals" poster

MCKENNA'S BAR AND BEAM

McKenna has her sights set on winning an Olympic gold medal one day. She knows she can achieve her dream if she works hard and believes in herself. McKenna spends all the time she can at the gym, perfecting her flips on the practice bar and rehearsing her tricky balance-beam routine.

Purple grips

Practice bar

Finding balance

McKenna uses the low-to-ground balance beam to learn new tricks. Giving her the confidence she needs, the practice beam helps McKenna perfect her moves before she tries them out on the higher beam.

★ American Girl

Reversible gym mat

ISABELLE'S STUDIO

When she's not practicing her ballet routines, Isabelle designs custom dancewear using her sewing machine, dress form, and a stock of beautiful embellishments. She loves bringing her ideas to life and creating eye-catching looks. Isabelle's studio has everything she needs to fuel her creative spirit.

DID YOU KNOW?
While her sister inspires Isabelle to dance her best, her mom—whose career is restoring antique textiles—inspires Isabelle's flair for fashion.

Storage pockets

Dress form

Inspirational fashion designs

Upholstered stool

Two-for-one space
The other side of Isabelle's studio features two mirrors and a ballet barre. Isabelle goes through positions at the barre and works on perfecting her dance routines.

GRACE'S BAKERY

Grace is delighted to visit her aunt and uncle's French bakery, called a *pâtisserie*, in Paris for the summer. Grace feels lucky to learn how to bake French pastries, cakes, and tarts in a professional bakery with state-of-the-art baking equipment.

French bakery sign

La Pâtisserie

Le Menu
Our delicious French
pastries and breads

Pâtisseries

Les macarons
Sweet meringue filled with creamy ganache

Mille-feuilles aux fraises
Strawberry-layered puff pastry with
vanilla-flavored cream

Plaisir sucré
Chocolate sheet layers with chocolate cream,
topped with a toasted hazelnut

Tarte au citron vert
Lime tart with marshmallow cream topping

Tarte au chocolat
Rich chocolate tart topped with a raspberry

Tarte aux framboises
Raspberry-filled custard tart

Pain au chocolat
Wand-rolled, flaky chocolate-filled croissant

Pains

Baguette parisienne
Long white loaf bread with a crispy crust

Pain aux olives
Long white loaf bread with olives

Chalkboard menu

Takeout boxes

Display shelf

On-the-go

Customers can eat their baked goods at the *pâtisserie*, or take them home to enjoy. Grace takes orders through the special window and serves up sweet treats to go.

DID YOU KNOW?
Grace takes inspiration from her aunt and uncle's Parisian bakery to set up her own pastry cart back home in Massachusetts.

Arched windows

Parisian treats

Monogrammed apron

Sidewalk café table

LEA'S RAINFOREST HOUSE

When Lea stays with her brother's host family deep in the Amazon jungle, she discovers the wonders of the Brazilian rainforest right outside her door. Lea is ready for a world of new sights and experiences—and she is ready to capture them all with her camera.

Jungle dwellers

Lea's favorite part of staying in the Amazon is seeing exotic animals. She spots many colorful butterflies and birds. On a hike through the rainforest, she finds an injured baby sloth.

Thatched roof

Loft bed

Hammock swing

Bamboo stilts

Tropical flower towel

Brick grill

Outdoor shower

GABRIELA'S STUDIO

DID YOU KNOW?
Gabriela's poetry group has a tradition: whenever someone shares a new poem, the group celebrates by shouting, "first draft!"

Gabriela loves to dance onstage, so she can't wait to perform her spoken-word poetry for an audience. Practicing in front of her poetry group in the studio gives Gabriela the confidence she needs to perform.

Practice mirror

LISTEN TO YOUR ART

In the studio
After dance practice, Gabriela takes some time to relax in the studio. She likes to listen to music to inspire her poetry.

Dance barre

Embroidered towel

★ American Girl
DANCE ★ STUDIO
STUDIO HOURS:
MONDAY-SATURDAY
10 AM - 9 PM

Z'S BEDROOM

Z is always on the lookout for a good story. She takes her camera wherever she goes, but her most creative work takes place in her bedroom. That's where she edits her footage into mini-movies.

Director's clapperboard

Light for filming

Laptop for editing

The POPCORN flip book

Time to edit

At her laptop, Z watches back her footage, chooses the best clips, and adds music and sounds to complete her film. Then she shares it with her family and friends.

TENNEY'S DRESSING ROOM

Before a show, Tenney gets ready in the dressing room backstage. After she's put on her best outfit and eaten a snack for energy, Tenney shines under the bright lights of the stage while she sings and plays her six-string guitar.

DID YOU KNOW?
The "on air" sign in her dressing room lets Tenney know that someone else is performing on stage.

Mirror with lights

ON AIR

LOVE DANCE SING

MUSIC

Good luck, Tenney!

Nashville

ROCK 'N' ROLL

Pre-show snacks

Satin robe

Tenney's tambourine

Tenney's backdrop

Stage light

INTRODUCING
TENNEY
NASHVILLE

Sing Your Story

Amplifier for Tenney's guitar

Microphone stand

Pre-show nerves

Although Tenney loves writing and playing her songs, she still gets nervous before a show. When she steps onstage, she takes a deep breath and imagines the people in the audience all wearing funny glasses!

Luciana's Mars habitat

Luciana is thrilled when she's invited to visit the Mars habitat in the Atacama Desert! There, she'll conduct experiments with NASA scientists and imagine that she's a real astronaut living on Mars, who will one day share her findings back on Earth.

DID YOU KNOW?
Luciana's invitation to the Mars habitat comes from Claire Jacobs, a teammate of hers at astronaut training camp.

Microscope

Space box for examining rocks

Rocks in a box

On Mars, some rocks might not be safe to handle. Luciana puts her hands through the openings of a "space box" to examine rocks safely.

Test tubes

Ladder

LUCIANA'S MAKER STATION

At Space Camp, Luciana and her teammates take part in a robotics competition. Their workstation gives them plenty of inspiration. But Luciana learns that building an inventive robot takes more than creativity and the right tools—it also takes teamwork.

DID YOU KNOW?
Luciana makes a mistake that destroys another team's robot, but she makes things right by helping to rebuild the robot.

Plant terrarium

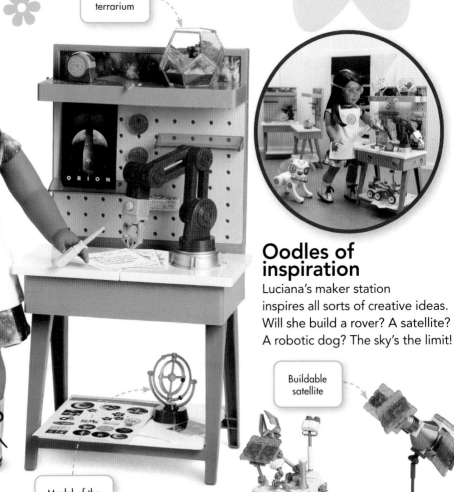

ORION

Oodles of inspiration

Luciana's maker station inspires all sorts of creative ideas. Will she build a rover? A satellite? A robotic dog? The sky's the limit!

Buildable satellite

Model of the solar system

Buildable rover

BLAIRE'S FAMILY FARM RESTAURANT

Blaire grew up cooking beside her mother and serving food to guests at her family's restaurant. She loves testing new recipes using fresh ingredients grown on the family farm. The best recipes end up on her blog, where she writes about all her cooking and farming adventures.

String lights

Four place settings

Order up
Blaire can cook yummy treats in the kitchen and pass them through the service window. A waiter then delivers the dishes to hungry guests.

DID YOU KNOW?
Pleasant View Farm is also a bed-and-breakfast, where Blaire helps to take care of guests during their stay.

Menus

Cart with serving tray

Dining table and benches

JOSS'S CHEER GYM

Walking into the cheer gym for the first time, Joss feels like a fish out of water. But she soon finds that the better she gets at cheer, the more her surfing improves, too. When a flyer on her team is out with an injury, Joss gets invited to step up into the role!

DID YOU KNOW?
Joss wears a headband at cheer practice to hold her hair back, but also to keep her hearing aid in place during tumbling.

Team spirit
Flying in cheer feels way different from launching off a wave into a surf trick. To be a great flyer in cheer, Joss has to rely on her teammates.

Stunt stand

Wedge mat

Team SHINE

Floor mat

KIRA'S EXAM ROOM

Kira longs to be like Aunt Mamie, a veterinarian who runs an animal clinic in Australia. Kira helps out in the exam room by bottle-feeding sick and injured joeys, or baby koalas, wombats, and kangaroos. Together, they nurse the animals back to health.

Blood pressure cuff

WILDLIFE RESCUE CLINIC

Stethoscope

Clipboard for notes

Koala care

Kira helps care for an adult koala named Mum. The koala, who is nearly blind, needs lots of eucalyptus leaves and love.

DID YOU KNOW?
The clinic has a room filled with wooden crates and soft blankets. It's a "joey nursery," meant only for baby animals.

KIRA'S PLATFORM TENT

While at the wildlife sanctuary, Kira sleeps in a bush camp with her new friend Alexis. The Wallaroo tent that they share is elevated on a platform. It has curtains for privacy and to keep the bugs out. Kira thinks it's amazing. It feels like it's in the middle of the wilderness!

At sunrise
Kira wakes at the crack of dawn in her tent, because she's not used to Australian time. When she can't sleep, she watches the sun rise.

Lantern

Sling-back chairs

Kangaroo pillow

Leaf-shaped plates

DID YOU KNOW?
Kira's tent is one of many at the bush camp. Other wildlife sanctuary workers—including Alexis's parents—sleep there, too!

Hanging mirror

Mosquito-net curtain

Wild Flowers of Australia

Koala pillow

Welcome

Welcome sign

Chapter 4
Girls on the go

How do girls explore their world? On bikes and in hot-air balloons. Paddling kayaks and cruising in campers. Wherever girls go, they make sure to enjoy the ride!

FELICITY'S CARRIAGE

When Felicity is invited to the Governor's Palace for a dancing lesson, she dresses in her finest gown. For such a special occasion, Felicity travels in a beautiful horse-drawn carriage. With soft tie-back curtains and lanterns to light the way, Felicity feels like a princess.

DID YOU KNOW?
Felicity's quilted bench seat lifts up to reveal a hidden storage compartment underneath. Felicity can keep secret treasures in her carriage.

A magical view
Felicity admires the snow-covered landscape as she travels to the Governor's Palace. It's a magical ride.

Fabric roof

Lanterns

Velvety curtains

Carriage poles

Bridle and reins

CAROLINE'S SKIFF

One of Caroline's favorite things to do is go sailing with her papa on Lake Ontario, especially in her very own boat. Papa repaired this wooden skiff and named it *Miss Caroline*. When Caroline sits inside and reaches for the oars, she feels right at home.

Into the sunset

During the day, Caroline shades her eyes with a wide-brimmed hat. When the sun sets over the lake, she takes off her hat and takes in the beautiful view.

DID YOU KNOW?
Caroline's papa built the two-seater boat himself at the family's shipyard.

Mast with canvas sail

Wooden oar

Painted name "Miss Caroline"

185

SAMANTHA'S BICYCLE

Uncle Gard gives Samantha a pretty pink bicycle and teaches her how to ride it in Grandmary's driveway. To make riding easier, Samantha wears checkered bloomers instead of a skirt, and black gaiters to cover her legs and keep her shoes clean. With her sun hat on, Samantha is ready to roll off on an adventure.

DID YOU KNOW?
On her first day of riding, Samantha swerves off the path and splashes into the lake! But she finds the courage to try again.

Woven basket

Bloomers

In the park
Once she gets the hang of riding, Samantha takes her bicycle to the park. Her dog, Jip, loves to run along beside her.

Gaiters

SAMANTHA AND NELLIE'S SLEIGH

One Christmas morning, Samantha and Nellie ride in a horse-drawn sleigh. The girls feel like they are in a magical winter wonderland as they glide over the snow with jingle bells ringing. It's chilly outside, but Samantha and Nellie keep warm under a cozy flannel blanket.

Holiday garland

Reins

DID YOU KNOW?
Nellie and Samantha glide through Central Park in New York City when they take their very first sleigh ride.

Jingle bells

Winter finery

Samantha and Nellie bundle up in beautiful new coats for their holiday sleigh ride. Their outfits are warm, stylish, and festive, too.

MARYELLEN'S SLED

Maryellen doesn't sled in sunny Florida. But when she visits her grandmom and grandpop in the mountains of Georgia, she sees snow for the very first time. Maryellen loves trying new things and blazing her own trail—even when it's straight down a sledding hill!

DID YOU KNOW?
Maryellen takes the train by herself to visit her grandparents over the holidays. She can't wait for her first snowy Christmas.

Faux fur-trimmed bonnet

Hitting the slopes

Maryellen can pull her sled uphill and then hop on for a ride back down. When she gets cold, she warms up with a hot drink.

Rope for pulling

Insulated drink container

Metal runners

JULIE'S BICYCLE

In 1976, Julie's neighborhood celebrates the United States Bicentennial, which marks 200 years since America declared that it would no longer be ruled by Great Britain. Decked out in red, white, and blue with patriotic stars on the wheels, Julie's banana-seat bike is the star of her neighborhood parade.

DID YOU KNOW?
Julie sometimes brings her pet rabbit, Nutmeg, along for the ride. He sits in the basket as Julie gently rolls through the neighborhood.

Fun on wheels
Julie gets a workout biking up and down the hilly streets of San Francisco. With her best friend by her side, Julie has fun, even on the steep hills!

Handlebar streamers

Star wheel decorations

Balancing kickstand

LANIE'S CAMPER

With her best friend far away in Indonesia working with baby orangutans, Lanie feels bored staying at home for the summer. When her aunt Hannah visits in her camper, Lanie jumps at the chance to go on an outdoor adventure.

DID YOU KNOW?
When weather doesn't allow Lanie to sleep under the stars, she can pull down the message board in the camper to create a bed.

Message board

Be Happy

USA

a seed is all you need

Storage bench

Door with window

Mini fridge

Tight spaces
Campers may look small, but they can fit a lot in a little space. Lanie's camper has a shower, mini fridge, stove, and even a hidden bed.

SAIGE'S HOT-AIR BALLOON

Saige feels lucky having a hot-air balloon pilot for a dad. It means she can soar into the sky above her home in Albuquerque, New Mexico. The amazing views inspire Saige's paintings. She also likes to take trips through the clouds with her grandmother Mimi.

Envelope (balloon)

Family fun
Saige prepares the basket before she and her dad take off into the picturesque New Mexican sky.

DID YOU KNOW?
Saige uses a map of Albuquerque and a pilot's logbook to help her dad track where they're flying and make notes about each of their flights.

Wicker basket

Opening door

LEA'S KAYAK

Lea is ready to explore all that Brazil has to offer, from its lush rainforests to its tropical beaches. She can't wait to take her kayak out on the water to see the colorful fish that swim beneath the waves!

Kayaking gear

Lea brings plenty of supplies with her when she goes kayaking. She can keep her mask and snorkel, waterproof camera, and sunscreen in the storage area behind her seat.

Sail that swivels

DID YOU KNOW?
Lea's kayak has a clear bottom, so she can see underwater without having to dive in.

Colorful paddle

Clear bottom

Z'S SCOOTER

With so much to capture on film, aspiring filmmaker Z often feels like she needs to be in two places at once. On her trusty scooter, she can zip around town in no time at all. The three-wheeled design means that Z can step off to make videos wherever inspiration takes her.

DID YOU KNOW?
Z often brings her dog, Popcorn, on filming trips around town. Popcorn loves to run alongside Z's scooter.

Striped helmet

Kneepads

Moving images

Z's scooter isn't just great for getting around; it can be a moving tripod, too. Attaching a camera to the front means that Z never misses a second of the action.

Z's Dalmatian, Popcorn

JOSS'S SURFBOARD

DID YOU KNOW?
Joss is also a skilled skateboarder. She can pop an ollie and catch air on her skateboard, too.

Surfing is Joss's happy place. She carves across the waves building speed and imagining that she's pro surfer Tina Hart. Her brother Dylan's camera attaches to the end of the board, so Joss can film her best aerial tricks!

Tina Hart's signature

Ready for action
When she gets to the beach, Joss rubs her surfboard with a bar of wax to help her feet grip the board. Then she hits the waves!

Ankle leash

KIRA'S ANIMAL CARRIER

When Kira and Aunt Mamie find lost or injured animals in the wildlife sanctuary, they bring them to the clinic in an animal carrier. Kira uses her walkie-talkie to let the clinic staff know they're on their way!

On the mend

Aunt Mamie, a veterinarian, treats animals at the clinic. Kira knows her favorite wombat is feeling better when he starts getting into mischief again!

Wombat tucked inside

Walkie-talkie

Wagon with handle

Historical characters

These characters have adventures based on important moments in the past. Their stories inspire girls of today to do their best and never let anything stand in the way of what's important to them.

Kaya™
1764

Felicity Merriman™
1774

Elizabeth Cole™
1775

Caroline Abbott™
1812

Josefina Montoya™
1824

Cécile Rey™
1853

Marie-Grace Gardner™1853

Kirsten Larson™
1854

Addy Walker™
1864

Samantha
Parkington™1904

Nellie O'Malley™
1906

Rebecca Rubin™
1914

Kit Kittredge™
1934

Ruthie Smithens™
1934

Nanea Mitchell™
1941

Molly McIntire™
1944

Emily Bennett™
1944

Maryellen Larkin™
1954

Melody Ellison™
1964

Julie Albright™
1974

Ivy Ling™
1974

Courtney Moore™
1986

Girl of the Year™ characters

These characters have the same interests and hobbies as today's girls—and face the same challenges, too. They inspire girls to aim high, be their best, and stand up for what matters.

Lindsey Bergman™
2001

Kailey Hopkins™
2003

Marisol Luna™
2005

Jess McConnell™
2006

Nicki Fleming™
2007

Mia St. Clair™
2008

Chrissa Maxwell™
2009

Sonali Matthews™
2009

Gwen Thompson™
2009

Lanie Holland™
2010

Kanani Akina™
2011

McKenna Brooks™
2012

Saige Copeland™
2013

Isabelle Palmer™
2014

Grace Thomas™
2015

Lea Clark™
2016

Gabriela McBride™
2017

Tenney Grant™
2017

Logan Everett™
2017

Z Yang™
2017

Luciana Vega™
2018

Blaire Wilson™
2019

Joss Kendrick™
2020

Kira Bailey™
2021

Animal friends

Animal friends come in all shapes and sizes. They can be furry, fuzzy, or even feathered. Pets make the perfect sidekicks, adding fun playtime and cozy cuddles whenever needed.

Kaya's Appaloosa, Steps High

Felicity's horse, Penny

Caroline's cat, Inkpot

Josefina's goat, Sombrita

Cécile's parrot, Cochon

Marie-Grace's dog, Argos

Kirsten's gray cat, Missy

Addy's canary, Sunny

Samantha's cocker spaniel, Jip

Rebecca's rescue kittens

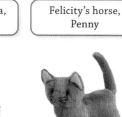

Kit's basset hound, Grace

Nanea's dog, Mele

Molly's terrier puppy, Bennett

Emily's terrier puppy, Yank

Maryellen's dachshund, Scooter

Melody's puppy, Bo

Julie's bunny, Nutmeg

Courtney's guinea pig, Parsley

Kailey's golden retriever, Sandy

Marisol's cat, Rascal

Nicki's dog, Sprocket

Nicki's buckskin horse, Jackson

Chrissa's llama, Starburst

Lanie's rabbit, Lulu

Lanie's woodland creatures

Kanani's dog, Barksee

McKenna's puppy, Cooper

Saige's horse, Picasso

Saige's Border Collie, Sam

Isabelle's white cat, Tutu

Grace's French bulldog, Bonbon

Luciana's robotic dog, Orion

Blaire's lamb, Penelope

Blaire's chicken, Dandelion

Joss's English bulldog, Murph

Kira's koala

Kira's wombat

Kira's kangaroo and joey

Historical accessories

Every character from the past comes with her own collection of historically accurate accessories. Through these accessories, girls of today can explore what life was like in days gone by.

Kaya's woven bag

Kaya's fringed saddle

Felicity's tea chair

Felicity's fashion doll

Elizabeth's fancy fan

Caroline's winter cap

Caroline's ice skates

Josefina's embroidered gold shawl

Josefina's weaving loom

Cécile's glass fruit bowl

Cécile's ribbon-and-floral mask

Marie-Grace's lacy parasol

Marie-Grace's vanity set

Kirsten's painted trunk

Kirsten's patchwork quilt

Addy's bean
doll, Ida

Addy's straw
bonnet

Samantha's basket
of tulips

Samantha's
tea set

Nellie's
drawstring bag

Rebecca's
dominoes

Rebecca's
phonograph

Kit's strawberry-
print apron

Ruthie's
slippers

Nanea's
ukulele

Nanea's lei

Molly's movie
popcorn

Molly's Miss Victory
costume

Emily's
wooden sled

Emily's ration
book

Maryellen's
poodle skirt

Maryellen's
TV set

Melody's
radio

Melody's
purse

Julie's
skateboard

Julie's knee-high
boots

Ivy's chocolate
fondue set

Ivy's purple
beret

Courtney's personal
cassette player

Courtney's cootie
catcher

Girl of the Year™ accessories

Whether it's dancing, painting, sports, or baking, every Girl of the Year™ has her own favorite hobby—and a whole host of exciting accessories to go with it!

Lindsey's laptop computer

Kailey's stand-up paddle board

Marisol's purple ballet slippers

Marisol's glittery rhinestone tiara

Jess's butterfly-shaped camera

Jess's tropical tankini

Nicki's Western-style hat

Nicki's snow goggles

Mia's walrus stuffed animal

Mia's accessory storage case

Chrissa's three-tiered cake

Chrissa's blue-green swimsuit

Sonali's knit tunic

Sonali's two-tone shoes

Gwen's eyelet-lace dress

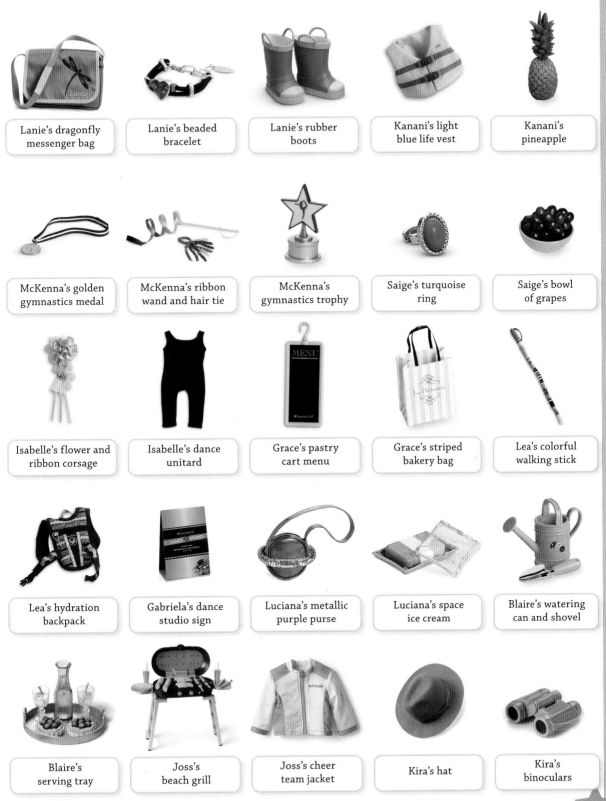

Lanie's dragonfly messenger bag

Lanie's beaded bracelet

Lanie's rubber boots

Kanani's light blue life vest

Kanani's pineapple

McKenna's golden gymnastics medal

McKenna's ribbon wand and hair tie

McKenna's gymnastics trophy

Saige's turquoise ring

Saige's bowl of grapes

Isabelle's flower and ribbon corsage

Isabelle's dance unitard

Grace's pastry cart menu

Grace's striped bakery bag

Lea's colorful walking stick

Lea's hydration backpack

Gabriela's dance studio sign

Luciana's metallic purple purse

Luciana's space ice cream

Blaire's watering can and shovel

Blaire's serving tray

Joss's beach grill

Joss's cheer team jacket

Kira's hat

Kira's binoculars

Index

Page numbers in **bold** refer to main entries.

Acknowledgments

Penguin Random House

Project Editor Lisa Stock
Senior Editor Laura Palosuo
Project Art Editor Jenny Edwards
Senior Designer Lisa Sodeau
Production Editor Siu Chan
Senior Production Controller Lloyd Robertson
Managing Editor Paula Regan
Design Manager Jo Connor
Publishing Director Mark Searle

This American Edition, 2021
First American Edition, 2017
Published in the United States by DK Publishing
1450 Broadway, Suite 801, New York, NY 10018

Page design copyright © 2021 Dorling Kindersley Limited

DK, a Division of Penguin Random House LLC

22 23 24 25 10 9 8 7 6 5 4 3

003–324663–Sep/21

© 2021 American Girl.
American Girl and associated trademarks
are owned by American Girl, LLC.

www.americangirl.com

Published in Great Britain by Dorling Kindersley Limited

A catalog record for this book
is available from the Library of Congress
ISBN 978-0-7440-4220-7

DK books are available at special discounts when
purchased in bulk for sales promotions, premiums,
fund-raising, or educational use.

For details, contact: DK Publishing Special Markets,
1450 Broadway, Suite 801, New York, NY 10018
SpecialSales@dk.com

Printed and bound in China

For the curious

www.dk.com
www.americangirl.com

DK would like to thank, Jodi Goldberg, Jennifer
Hirsch, Molly Schlichting, and Wendy Walsh at
American Girl, and Ryan Ferguson at Mattel.

DK would also like to thank Lori Hand for proofreading.

MIX
Paper from
responsible sources
FSC www.fsc.org **FSC™ C018179**

This book was made with Forest
Stewardship Council ™ certified
paper—one small step in DK's
commitment to a sustainable
future. For more information go to
www.dk.com/our-green-pledge